Working Papers

for use with

FUNDAMENTAL
ACCOUNTING PRINCIPLES

LARSON | JENSEN

FOURTEENTH CANADIAN EDITION | VOLUME 1

Prepared by Tilly Jensen

Revised by Susan Hurley, Wendy Popowich, Ruby So Koumarelas,
and reviewed by Joan Baines

Working Papers

for use with

FUNDAMENTAL
ACCOUNTING PRINCIPLES

LARSON | JENSEN

FOURTEENTH CANADIAN EDITION | VOLUME 1

Kermit D. Larson

University of Texas – Austin

Tilly Jensen

Athabasca University – Alberta

Prepared by Tilly Jensen

Revised by Susan Hurley, Wendy Popowich, Ruby So Koumarelas,
and reviewed by Joan Baines

**McGraw-Hill
Ryerson**
Connect. Learn. Succeed.

**Working Papers for use with
Fundamental Accounting Principles
Fourteenth Canadian Edition
Volume 1**

ISBN-13: 978-0-07-093207-4
ISBN-10: 0-07-093207-7

5 6 7 8 9 10 MP 1 9 8 7 6 5

Printed and bound in Canada.

Director of Product Management: Rhondda McNabb
Product Manager: Keara Emmett
Executive Marketing Manager: Joy Armitage Taylor
Product Developer: Suzanne Simpson Millar
Supervising Editor: Jessica Barnoski
Production Coordinator: Tammy Mavroudi
Cover Design: Greg Devitt
Page Layout: Brian Lehen Graphic Design Ltd.
Printer: Maracle Press, Ltd.

Contents

Quick Study 1-1

Quick Study 1-2

a.

b.

c.

d.

Quick Study 1-3

a. Highlands United Church (Non-business)
b. Royal Alexandra Hospital (Non-business)
c. RBC (Business)
d. CDI College (Business)
e. Loblaw (Business)
f. World Vision (Non-business)

Quick Study 1-4

Quick Study 1-4 (concl'd)

Quick Study 1-5

Quick Study 1-6

Quick Study 1-7

a. Business entity principle

b. Revenue recognition principle

c. Cost principle

Quick Study 1-8

1. Revenue Recognition   4. Going Concern

2. Cost   5. Monetary Unit

3. Business Entity

Quick Study 1-9

Monetary Unit	a.	Delco performed work for a client located in China and collected 8,450,000 RMB (Chinese currency), the equivalent of about $1,320,000 Canadian. Delco recorded it as 8,450,000.
Revenue Recognition	b.	Delco collected $180,000 from a customer on December 20, 2014, for work to be done in February, 2015. The $180,000 was recorded as revenue during 2011. Delco's year end is December 31.
Going Concern	c.	Delco's December 31, 2014, balance sheet showed total assets of $840,000 and liabilities of $1,120,000. The income statement for the past 6 years has shown a trend of increasing losses.
Cost	d.	Included in Delco's assets was land and building purchased for $310,000 and reported on the balance sheet at $470,000.
Business Entity	e.	Delco's owner, Tom Del, consistently buys personal supplies and charges them to the company.

Quick Study 1-10

1. SP   5. C

2. C   6. C

3. D   7. D

4. SP

Quick Study 1-11

	Assets	=	Liabilities	+	Equity
a.	$75,000		$40,500		$34,500
b.	$300,000		$214,500		$85,500
c.	$28,900		$187,500		$95,400

Quick Study 1-12

	Assets	=	Liabilities	+	Equity
a.	374,700		252,450		122,250
b.	150,900		126,000		24,900
c.	37,650		112,500		150,150

Quick Study 1-13

a.

Allin Servicing Income Statement For Month Ended April 30, 2014	
Revenues	$300
Expenses..................................	125?
Net income (loss)	175?

Allin Servicing Statement of Changes in Equity For Month Ended April 30, 2014		
Tim Allin, capital, April 1		$ 50
Add: Investments by owner	$ 30	
Net income..............................	175?	205?
Total......................................		$255
Less: Withdrawals by owner.........		15?
Tim Allin, capital, April 30.............		$240?

Allin Servicing Balance Sheet April 30, 2014			
Assets		**Liabilities**	
Cash............ $ 60		Accounts payable $ 25	
Equipment... 205?		**Equity**	
		Tim Allin, capital 240 ?	
		Total liabilities	
Total assets .. $265		and equity $265?	

b.

Servicing Income Statement For Month Ended May 31, 2014	
Revenues	?
Expenses..................................	$ 85
Net income (loss)	?

Allin Servicing Statement of Changes in Equity For Month Ended May 31, 2014		
Tim Allin, capital, May 1		?
Add: Investments by owner	$ 60	
Net income..............................	?	$110
Total......................................		?
Less: Withdrawals by owner.........		75
Tim Allin, capital, May 31		?

Allin Servicing Balance Sheet May 31, 2014			
Assets		**Liabilities**	
Cash............ $120		Accounts payable $ 45	
Equipment... ?		**Equity**	
		Tim Allin, capital ?	
		Total liabilities	
Total assets .. ?		and equity ?	

Quick Study 1-14

1. _____

2. _____

Quick Study 1-15

_____ a. Income statement

_____ b. Statement of cash flows

_____ c. Telephone bill

_____ d. Invoice from supplier

_____ e. Owner's withdrawals account

_____ f. Balance sheet

_____ g. Bank statement

_____ h. Sales invoice

Quick Study 1-16

	Assets	=	Liabilities	+	Equity
a.	Increase/Decrease				
b.	Increase		Increase		
c.	Decrease		Decrease		
d.			Increase		Decrease
e.	Decrease				Decrease

Quick Study 1-17

___C___ 1. Supplies   ___a___ 8. Utilities expense

___a___ 2. Supplies expense   ___C___ 9. Furniture

___C___ 3. Accounts receivable   ___a___ 10. Fees earned

___C___ 4. Accounts payable   ___a___ 11. Rent revenue

___C___ 5. Equipment   ___a___ 12. Salaries expense

___b___ 6. Tim Roadster's withdrawals   ___b___ 13. Tim Roadster's investments

___C___ 7. Notes payable   ___a,b___ 14. Net income

Quick Study 1-18

$70+35=105$ 1. Total revenues

$22+10+45=77$ 2. Total operating expenses

$105-77-28$ 3. Net income

$10+25+40+20=95$ 4. Total assets

$12+30=42$ 5. Total liabilities

$60-35+28=53$ 6. Tim Roadster, capital (April 30, 2014)

$42+53=95$ 7. Total liabilities and equity

Quick Study 1-19

d	1.	Net loss	$ 2
d	2.	Rent expense	22
b	3.	Rent payable	6
a	4.	Accounts receivable	14
d	5.	Joan Bennish's investments in May	30
d	6.	Interest revenue	2
d	7.	Joan Bennish, capital, May 1, 2014	0
a	8.	Repair supplies	5
b	9.	Notes payable	25
d	10.	Joan Bennish's withdrawals in May	5
a	11.	Truck	15
d	12.	Consulting fees earned	18
c	13.	Joan Bennish, capital, May 31, 2014	
a	14.	Cash	20

Income Statement
Income Statement

Quick Study 1-20

Income Statement		

Statement of Changes in Equity		

Balance Sheet			

*Name*_____

Exercise 1-1

a. _____
b. _____
c. _____
d. _____
e. _____
f. _____
g. _____

Exercise 1-2

	I or E		*I or E*
Bank manager		Parent	
Owner		Canada Revenue Agency	
Toy supplier		Cleaner contracted by TLC Daycare	

Exercise 1-3

1. _____
2. _____
3. _____
4. _____
5. _____
6. _____
7. _____
8. _____

Chapter 1

*Name*_____

Exercise 1-4

a.

_____

_____

_____

_____

_____

_____

_____

_____

_____

_____

b.

_____

_____

_____

_____

_____

_____

_____

_____

_____

_____

_____

c.

_____

_____

_____

_____

_____

_____

_____

_____

_____

_____

Chapter 1   *Name*_____

Exercise 1-5

1. _____
2. _____
3. _____
4. _____

Exercise 1-6

a. _____
b. _____
c. _____
_____
d. _____
_____
_____
_____

Exercise 1-7

	(a)	(b)	(c)	(d)	(e)
Equity, January 1	$ -0-	$ -0-	$ -0-	$ -0-	
Owner's investments during the year	60,000		31,500	37,500	140,000
Net income (loss) for the year	15,750	30,500	(4,500)		(8,000)
Owner's withdrawals during the year		(27,000)	(20,000)	(15,750)	(63,000)
Equity, December 31.......................	56,000	49,500		32,000	171,000

Exercise 1-8

Income Statement		

Exercise 1-9

Statement of Changes in Equity		

Analysis component:

_____

_____

_____

_____

Exercise 1-10

	Balance Sheet		

Analysis component:

_____

_____

_____

_____

Exercise 1-11

	Income Statement	

Exercise 1-12

	Statement of Changes in Equity	

Analysis component:

_____

_____

_____

_____

Name_____

Exercise 1-13

Balance Sheet

Analysis component:

_____

_____

_____

_____

Exercise 1-14

(a) Net Income (Loss) = [ ]
    Supporting Calculations: _____
_____
_____
_____
_____
_____
_____

(b) Net Income (Loss) = [ ]
    Supporting Calculations: _____
_____
_____
_____
_____
_____

(c) Net Income (Loss) = [ ]
    Supporting Calculations: _____
_____
_____
_____
_____
_____

(d) Net Income (Loss) = [ ]
    Supporting Calculations: _____
_____
_____
_____
_____
_____

Exercise 1-15

(a) **Assets =**
   Equity =
   Supporting Calculations:

_____
_____
_____
_____
_____

(b) **Liabilities =**
   Equity =
   Supporting Calculations:

_____
_____
_____
_____
_____

Exercise 1-16

	ASSETS			=	LIABILITIES	+	EQUITY
CASH	+	ACCOUNTS RECEIVABLE	+ OFFICE SUPPLIES	=	ACCOUNTS PAYABLE	+	MARNIE WESSON, CAPITAL
(a)							
(b)							
(c)							
(d)							
(e)							
(f)							

Chapter 1

Name_____

Exercise 1-17

	CASH +	ACCOUNTS RECEIVABLE +	PARTS SUPPLIES +	EQUIPMENT =	ACCOUNTS PAYABLE +	STACEY CROWE, CAPITAL
	ASSETS				**= LIABILITIES**	**+ EQUITY**
(a)	+14,000					+14,000
(b)	−2500					−2500
(c)			+800		+800	
(d)	+3,400					+3,400
(e)	−1,950			+1,950		
(f)	—					
(g)	−800				−800	
(h)	+3,400					+3,400
(i)	−2,700					−2,700

9450 + 3,400 + 800 + 1950 + (0 + 15,600

(15,600)   (15,600

Exercise 1-18

a. _____
b. _____
c. _____
d. _____
e. _____
f. _____
g. _____

	ASSETS			=	LIABILITIES	+	EQUITY	
CASH	+ ACCOUNTS RECEIVABLE	+ SUPPLIES	+ EQUIP- MENT	=	ACCOUNTS PAYABLE	+	MAILIN MOON, CAPITAL	EXPLANATION OF EQUITY TRANSACTION
(a)								
(b)								
(c)								
(d)								
(e)								
(f)								
(g)								

Name_____

Exercise 1-20

Mailin Moon – Freelance Writing
Income Statement
For Month Ended March 31, 2014

Revenues:
    Freelance writing revenue ....
Operating expenses:
    Salaries expense ....
    Rent expense...
        Total operating expenses ....
Net income..

Mailin Moon – Freelance Writing
Statement of Changes in Equity
For Month Ended March 31, 2014

Mailin Moon, capital, March 1 ....
Add: Investment by owner..
        Net income..
Mailin Moon, capital, March 31 ....

Mailin Moon – Freelance Writing
Balance Sheet
March 31, 2014

      Assets

                                    Liabilities
Cash ....   Accounts payable ....
Accounts receivable .
Supplies ....
Equipment.................

                                           Equity
                                Mailin Moon, capital ....
Total assets ....   Total liabilities and equity ....

Analysis component:

_____
_____
_____
_____
_____
_____
_____

Exercise 1-21

		ASSETS			=	LIABILITIES	+	EQUITY	
CASH	+	ACCOUNTS RECEIVABLE	+	SUPPLIES	+	EQUIP- MENT	=	ACCOUNTS PAYABLE	+	PETE KEQUAHTOO WAY, CAPITAL	EXPLANATION OF EQUITY TRANSACTION
(a)									
(b)									
(c)									
(d)									
(e)									
(f)									
(g)									
(h)									
(i)									

Exercise 1-22

Income Statement

Statement of Changes in Equity

Name_____

Balance Sheet

Analysis component:

_____

_____

_____

_____

_____

_____

_____

_____

Exercise 1-23

		ASSETS			=	LIABILITIES	+	EQUITY	
CASH	+	ACCOUNTS RECEIVABLE	+ SUPPLIES +	EQUIP- MENT	= ACCOUNTS PAYABLE	+	OTTO INGLES, CAPITAL	EXPLANATION OF EQUITY TRANSACTION
Bal.$6,000		$1,200	$1,900	$6,500	$4,000		$11,600	
(a)								
(b)								
(c)								
(d)								
(e)								
(f)								
(g)								
(h)								

Exercise 1-24

Income Statement

Statement of Changes in Equity

Balance Sheet

Analysis component:

*Name*_____

Problem 1-1A

Characteristic	Type of Business Organization		
	Sole Proprietorship	Partnership	Corporation
Limited liability			
Unlimited liability			
Owners are shareholders			
Owners are partners			
Taxed as a separate legal entity			

Problem 1-2A

2013 Net Income (Loss) = [   ]
      Supporting Calculations: _____

_____

_____

_____

_____

_____

_____

_____

_____

_____

_____

Name_____

Problem 1-3A

Income Statement

Statement of Changes in Equity

Name_____

Problem 1-3A (concl'd.)

Balance Sheet

Analysis component:

_____
_____
_____
_____
_____

Problem 1-4A

Part 1

Balance Sheet

Name_____

Problem 1-4A (concl'd.)

Balance Sheet

Part 2

Net Income (Loss) Calculation:

_____
_____
_____
_____
_____
_____
_____
_____
_____
_____
_____

Analysis component:

_____
_____
_____
_____
_____
_____
_____
_____
_____

Name_____

Problem 1-5A

Part 1: Company A

(a) _____
_____
_____
_____

(b) _____
_____
_____
_____
_____
_____
_____

(c) _____
_____
_____
_____
_____

Part 2: Company B

(a) _____
_____
_____
_____

(b) _____
_____
_____
_____
_____

(c) _____
_____
_____
_____

*Name*_____

Problem 1-5A (cont'd.)

Part 3: Company C

_____
_____
_____
_____
_____
_____
_____
_____
_____
_____
_____
_____
_____
_____

Part 4: Company D

_____
_____
_____
_____
_____
_____
_____
_____
_____
_____
_____
_____
_____
_____
_____
_____
_____
_____

Problem 1-5A (concl'd.)

Part 5: Company E

_____
_____
_____
_____
_____
_____
_____

_____
_____
_____
_____
_____
_____
_____

Name _____

Parts 1 and 2

	CASH	+	ACCOUNTS RECEIVABLE	+	OFFICE SUPPLIES	+	OFFICE EQUIPMENT	+	BUILDING	=	ACCOUNTS PAYABLE	+	NOTES PAYABLE	+	GEORGE LITTLECHILD, CAPITAL	EXPLANATION OF EQUITY TRANSACTION
			ASSETS							=	LIABILITIES				EQUITY	
(a)	160,000						20,000								$180,000	Investment by owner
(b)	100,000								600,000				500,000			
Bal.																
(c)	3,000				3,000											
Bal.	143,000															
(d)							72,000				72,000					
Bal.																
(e)																
Bal.																
(f)	5,200		5,200												5,200	Service Revenue
Bal.																
(g)	3,500										3,500				3,500	Advertising Expense
Bal.																
(h)	4,000										4,000				4,000	Service Revenue
Bal.																
(i)	4,000										4,000					
Bal.																
(j)	2,500		2,500													
Bal.																
(k)	7,000														7,000	Wages Expense
Bal.																
(l)	3,600														3,600	Withdrawal by owner
Bal.	45,400 + 2,700 + 3,000 + 3,000 + 72,000 + 600,000 = 98,000 + 500,000 + 175,100															

$$(743,100) \qquad (743,100)$$

Problem 1-6A (concl'd.)

Littlechild Enterprises
Income Statement
For Month Ended March 31, 2014

Revenues :
    Service revenue..
Operating expenses:
    Wages expense ....
    Advertising expense 3,500
        Total operating expenses ....
Net loss.. 1,300

Littlechild Enterprises
Statement of Changes in Equity
For Month Ended March 31, 2014

George Littlechild, capital, March 1
Add: Investment by owner   180,000
    Total
Less: Withdrawal by owner
        Net loss   1,300
George Littlechild, capital, March 31   175,100

Littlechild Enterprises
Balance Sheet
March 31, 2014

Assets	**Liabilities**	
Cash	Accounts payable	
Accounts receivable	Notes payable	500,000
Office supplies	Total liabilities	
Office equipment		
Building		
	Equity	
	George Littlechild, capital	175,100
Total assets 743,100	Total liabilities and equity	743,100

Analysis component:

568,000/743,100 ×100 = 76.44 % or 76%.

_____
_____
_____
_____
_____

Name __Sabreen. Sidhu__

DATE	CASH	+ ACCOUNTS RECEIVABLE	+ OFFICE SUPPLIES	+ OFFICE EQUIPMENT	+ ELECTRICAL EQUIPMENT	= ACCOUNTS PAYABLE	+ LARRY POWER, CAPITAL	EXPLANATION OF EQUITY TRANSACTION
Oct 31	30,000	1,000	1,900	28,000	14,000	18,000	62,900	
Nov 1	-7,200						-7,200	Rent expense
Nov 3	+10,000						10,000	Investment by owner
Nov 3	-10,000				16,000	6,000		
Nov 5	-1,800		1,800					
Nov 6	+2,000							
Nov 8				5,200		5,200	2,000	Electrical fees earned
Nov 15		6,000					6,000	Electrical fees earned
Nov 16							6,000	Electrical fees earned
Nov 18			1,000			1,000		
Nov 20	-5,200					5,200		
Nov 24		4,800					4,800	Electrical fees earned
Nov 28	6,000	6,000						
Nov 30	4,400						4400	Salaries expense
Nov 30	3,600						3,660	Utilities expense
Nov 30	400						1,400	Withdrawal by owner

Name_____

Problem 1-7A (concl'd.)

Analysis component:

_____
_____
_____
_____
_____
_____

Problem 1-8A

Income Statement

Statement of Changes in Equity

Name_____

Problem 1-8A (concl'd.)

Balance Sheet

Analysis component:

_____

_____

_____

_____

_____

Problem 1-9A

		BALANCE SHEET			INCOME STATEMENT
	TRANSACTION	TOTAL ASSETS	TOTAL LIABILITIES	EQUITY	NET INCOME
1.	Owner invests cash				
2.	Sell services for cash				
3.	Acquire services on credit				
4.	Pay wages with cash				
5.	Owner withdraws cash				
6.	Borrow cash with note payable				
7.	Sell services on credit				
8.	Buy office equipment for cash				
9.	Collect receivable from (7)				
10.	Buy asset with note payable				

*Name*_____

Problem 1-1B

a._____
_____
_____

b._____
_____
_____

Problem 1-2B

2013 Net Income (Loss) =   [   ]
    Supporting Calculations:_____
_____
_____
_____
_____
_____
_____
_____
_____

Problem 1-3B

_____

Income Statement

Problem 1-3B (concl'd.)

Statement of Changes in Equity

Balance Sheet

Analysis component:

_____

_____

_____

_____

_____

_____

Problem 1-4B   **Part 1**

Balance Sheet			

Balance Sheet			

Problem 1-4B (concl'd.)

Part 2

Net Income (Loss) Calculation:

Analysis component:

Problem 1-5B

Part 1: Company V

(a)

(b)

(c)

Name_____

Problem 1-5B (cont'd.)

Part 2: Company W

(a) _____
_____
_____
_____

(b) _____
_____
_____
_____
_____
_____
_____

(c) _____
_____
_____
_____
_____
_____

Part 3: Company X

_____
_____
_____
_____
_____
_____
_____
_____
_____
_____
_____
_____
_____
_____
_____

Name_____

Problem 1-5B (concl'd.)

Part 4: Company Y

_____
_____
_____
_____
_____
_____
_____
_____
_____
_____
_____
_____
_____
_____

Part 5: Company Z

_____
_____
_____
_____
_____
_____
_____
_____
_____
_____
_____
_____
_____
_____
_____
_____
_____
_____
_____
_____

Name_____

Problem 1-6B (Parts 1 and 2)

	ASSETS					=	LIABILITIES		+	EQUITY	
	CASH	+ ACCOUNTS RECEIVABLE	+ OFFICE SUPPLIES	+ OFFICE EQUIPMENT	+ BUILDING	=	ACCOUNTS PAYABLE	+ NOTES PAYABLE	+	LILY COE, CAPITAL	EXPLANATION OF EQUITY TRANSACTION
(a)											
(b)											
Bal.											
(c)											
Bal.											
(d)											
Bal.											
(e)											
Bal.											
(f)											
Bal.											
(g)											
Bal.											
(h)											
Bal.											
(i)											
Bal.											
(j)											
Bal.											
(k)											
Bal.											
(l)											
Bal.											

Problem 1-6B (concl'd.)

Coe Consulting
Income Statement
For Year Ended December 31, 2014

Revenues:
Consulting services revenue..................................
Operating expenses:
Wages expense ....
Advertising expense ....   _____
Total operating expenses ....
Net income...

Coe Consulting
Statement of Changes in Equity
For Year Ended December 31, 2014

Lily Coe, capital, January 1
Add: Investment by owner
Net income
Total
Less: Withdrawals by owner
Lily Coe, capital, December 31

Coe Consulting
Balance Sheet
December 31, 2014

Assets		Liabilities	
Cash		Accounts payable	
Accounts receivable		Notes payable	
Office supplies		Total liabilities	
Office equipment			
Building			
		Equity	
		Lily Coe, capital	
Total assets		Total liabilities and equity	

Analysis component:

_____

_____

_____

_____

_____

_____

_____

_____

| DATE | ASSETS | | | | | LIABILITIES | EQUITY | |
	CASH	+ ACCOUNTS RECEIVABLE	+ OFFICE SUPPLIES	+ OFFICE EQUIPMENT	+ EXCAVATING EQUIPMENT	= ACCOUNTS PAYABLE	+ ROBERT CANTU, CAPITAL	EXPLANATION OF EQUITY TRANSACTION

Name_____

Analysis component:

_____
_____
_____
_____
_____
_____
_____

Problem 1-8B

Income Statement

Statement of Changes in Equity

Problem 1-8B (concl'd.)

Balance Sheet

Analysis component:

_____
_____
_____
_____
_____
_____
_____

Problem 1-9B

	TRANSACTION	BALANCE SHEET			INCOME STATEMENT
		TOTAL ASSETS	TOTAL LIABILITIES	EQUITY	NET INCOME
1.	Owner invests cash				
2.	Pay wages with cash				
3.	Acquire services on credit				
4.	Buy store equipment for cash				
5.	Borrow cash with note payable				
6.	Sell services for cash				
7.	Sell services on credit				
8.	Pay rent with cash				
9.	Owner withdraws cash				
10.	Collect receivable from (7)				

1.	A	Buildings	16.	L	Unearned Subscription Fees
2.	E	Building Repair Expense	17.	A	Prepaid Subscription Fees
3.	E	Wages Expense	18.	A	Supplies
4.	L	Wages Payable	19.	E	Supplies Expense
5.	A	Notes Receivable	20.	R	Rent Revenue
6.	L	Notes Payable	21.	L	Unearned Rent Revenue
7.	A	Prepaid Advertising	22.	A	Prepaid Rent
8.	E	Advertising Expense	23.	L	Rent Payable
9.	L	Advertising Payable	24.	A	Service Fees Earned
10.	L	Unearned Advertising	25.	W	Jan Sted, Withdrawals
11.	R	Advertising Fees Earned	26.	OE	Jan Sted, Capital
12.	R	Interest Earned	27.	E	Salaries Expense
13.	E	Interest Expense	28.	L	Salaries Payable
14.	L	Interest Payable	29.	A	Furniture
15.	R	Earned Subscription Fees	30.	A	Equipment

Quick Study 2-2

Accounts Receivable

1,000	650
400	920
920	1,500
3,000	
2550	

Accounts Payable

250	250
900	1,800
650	1,400
	650
	2300

Service Revenue

	13,000
	2,500
	810
	3,500
	19810

Utilities Expense

610
520
390
275
1795

Cash

3,900	2,400
17,800	3,900
14,500	21,800
340	
8440	

Notes Payable

4,000	50,000
8,000	
	38000

a. __D__ Equipment
b. __D__ Land
c. __D__ Al Tait, Withdrawals
d. __D__ Rent Expense
e. __C__ Interest Revenue
f. __D__ Prepaid Rent
g. __D__ Accounts Receivable
h. __D__ Office Supplies

i. __D__ Notes Receivable
j. __C__ Notes Payable
k. __C__ Al Tait, Capital
l. __C__ Rent Earned
m. __C__ Rent Payable
n. __D__ Interest Expense
o. __C__ Interest Payable

Quick Study 2-4

a. __C__ To increase Notes Payable
b. __C__ To decrease Accounts Rec'ble.
c. __C__ To increase Owner, Capital
d. __D__ To decrease Unearned Fees
e. __C__ To decrease Prepaid Insurance
f. __C__ To decrease Cash
g. __D__ To increase Utilities Expense
h. __D__ To increase Fees Earned

i. __D__ To increase Store Equip.
j. __D__ To increase Owner, With.
k. __D__ To decrease Rent Payable
l. __C__ To decrease Prepaid Rent
m. __D__ To increase Supplies
n. __D__ To increase Supplies Exp.
o. __D__ To decrease Accts. Payable

Quick Study 2-5

a. __C__ Buildings
b. __D__ Interest Revenue
c. __C__ Bob Norton, Withdrawals
d. __D__ Bob Norton, Capital
e. __C__ Prepaid Insurance
f. __D__ Interest Payable
g. __C__ Accounts Receivable
h. __C__ Salaries Expense

i. __C__ Office Supplies
j. __D__ Repair Services Revenue
k. __C__ Interest Expense
l. __D__ Unearned Revenue
m. __D__ Salaries Payable
n. __C__ Furniture
o. _____ Interest Receivable

Quick Study 2-6

a. __173__ Buildings *A*
b. __409__ Interest Revenue *E*
c. __302__ Bob Norton, Withdrawals *OE*
d. __301__ Bob Norton, Capital *OE*
e. __128__ Prepaid Insurance *A*
f. __203__ Interest Payable *L*
g. __106__ Accounts Receivable *A*
h. __622__ Salaries Expense *E*

i. __124__ Office Supplies *A*
j. __403__ Repair Services Revenue *OE*
k. __633__ Interest Expense *L*
l. __232__ Unearned Revenue *L*
m. __207__ Salaries Payable *L*
n. __161__ Furniture *A*
o. __109__ Interest Receivable *A*

Cash	101
(a) 15,000	500
(d) 1,000	500
(g) 300	
15,300	

Accounts Receivable	106
700	300
400	

Furniture	161
(b) 2,000	
(c) 500	
2500	

Accounts Payable	201
500	2000
	1,500

Del Martin, Capital	301
	15,000
	15,000

Revenue	403
	1000
	400
	700
	2100

Part 2

$$18,000 = 1,500 + 17,100$$

_____

_____

_____

Cash	101		
Apr. 30	15,000	6000	May 5
May 12	10,000	8000	May 22
May 16	4000		
	20,000		

Accounts Receivable	106		
Apr. 30	3,200	4000	May 16
May 10	4000		
	3200		

Car	150
May 2 –8,000	

Accounts Payable	202		
May 22	3000	6,000	Apr. 30

Unearned Revenue	205		
		1,800	Apr. 30
		10,000	May 12
		11,800	

Dee Bell, Capital	301		
		8,900	Apr. 30
		8000	May 2
		16,900	

Revenue	410		
		3,000	Apr. 30
		4000	May 10
		7000	

Wages Expense	650	
Apr. 30	1,500	
May 15	6000	
	7500	

Part 3

$$31,000 = 14,800 + 16,400$$

_____
_____
_____

GENERAL JOURNAL   Page _____

Date	Account Titles and Explanation	PR	Debit	Credit
May 1	Equipment		500	
	Accounts Payable			500
2)	Accounts Payable		500	
	Cash			500
3)	Supplies		100	
	Cash			100
4)	Wages Expense		2000	
	Cash			2000
5	Cash		750	
	Service Revenue			750
6	Account Receivable		2500	
	Service Revenue			2500
7	Cash		2500	
	Accounts Receivable			2500

GENERAL JOURNAL

Jan

Date	Account Titles and Explanation	PR	Debit	Credit
3	Cash	101	60,000	
	Equipment	167	40,000	
	Stan Adams, Capital	301		
4	Office Supplies	124	340	
	Accounts Payable	201		340
6	Cash	101	5,200	
	Landscaping Services Revenue	403		5,200
15	Accounts Payable	201	200	
	Cash	101		200
16	Office Supplies	124	700	
	Accounts Payable	201		700
30	Accounts Payable	201	140	
	Cash	101		140

Cash   ACCOUNT NO. ____

DATE	EXPLANATION	PR	DEBIT	CREDIT	BALANCE
3			60,000		60,000
6			5,200		65,200
15				200	65,000
30				140	64,860

Office Supplies   ACCOUNT NO. ____

DATE	EXPLANATION	PR	DEBIT	CREDIT	BALANCE
4			340		340
16			700		1,040

Equipment   ACCOUNT NO. ____

DATE	EXPLANATION	PR	DEBIT	CREDIT	BALANCE
3			40,000		40,000

Accounts Payable   ACCOUNT NO. ____

DATE	EXPLANATION	PR	DEBIT	CREDIT	BALANCE
4				340	340
15			200		140
16				700	840
30			140		700

Stan Adams, Capital   ACCOUNT NO. ____

DATE	EXPLANATION	PR	DEBIT	CREDIT	BALANCE
3				100,000	100,000

Landscaping Services Revenue   ACCOUNT NO. ____

DATE	EXPLANATION	PR	DEBIT	CREDIT	BALANCE
6				5,200	5,200

Trial Balance

	Debit	Credit
Cash	7,000	
Equipment	9,000	
Unearned fees		2000
Brea Vahn, Capital		14,000
Brea Vahn, withdrawals	1,000	
Fees earned		11,000
Rent expense	6000	
Utilities	4000	
Total	27,000	27,000

Quick Study 2-13

_____
_____
_____
_____
_____

Quick Study 2-14

_____
_____
_____
_____
_____
_____
_____

Quick Study 2-15

_____
_____
_____
_____
_____
_____
_____
_____

Cash		Accounts Receivable

		Office Supplies

Office Equipment		Accounts Payable

Sandra Moses, Capital		Sandra Moses, Withdrawals

Fees Earned		Rent Expense

	Cash				Accounts Receivable	
Bal.	890			Bal.	1,200	

	Prepaid Insurance	
Bal.	-0-	

	Computer Equipment				Accounts Payable	
Bal.	480				250	Bal.

	Notes Payable				Neil Poundmaker, Capital	
	-0-	Bal.			800	Bal.

	Neil Poundmaker, Withdrawals				Service Revenue	
Bal.	-0-				2,600	Bal.

	Wages Expense	
Bal.	1,080	

Analysis component:

_____
_____
_____
_____
_____
_____
_____
_____
_____
_____

Cash	
Bal. 1,800	

Accounts Receivable	
Bal. 4,800	

Repair Supplies	
Bal. 1,400	

Equipment	
Bal. 7,400	

Accounts Payable	
	500 Bal.

Nels Sigurdsen, Capital	
	2,350 Bal.

Nels Sigurdsen, Withdrawals	
Bal. 500	

Repair Revenue	
	14,000 Bal.

Rent Expense	
Bal. 950	

Exercise 2-4 (add part 2)

Parts 1 and 3

Note: T-accounts may be used or the balance column format; both are provided for in Parts 1 and 3 of this exercise.

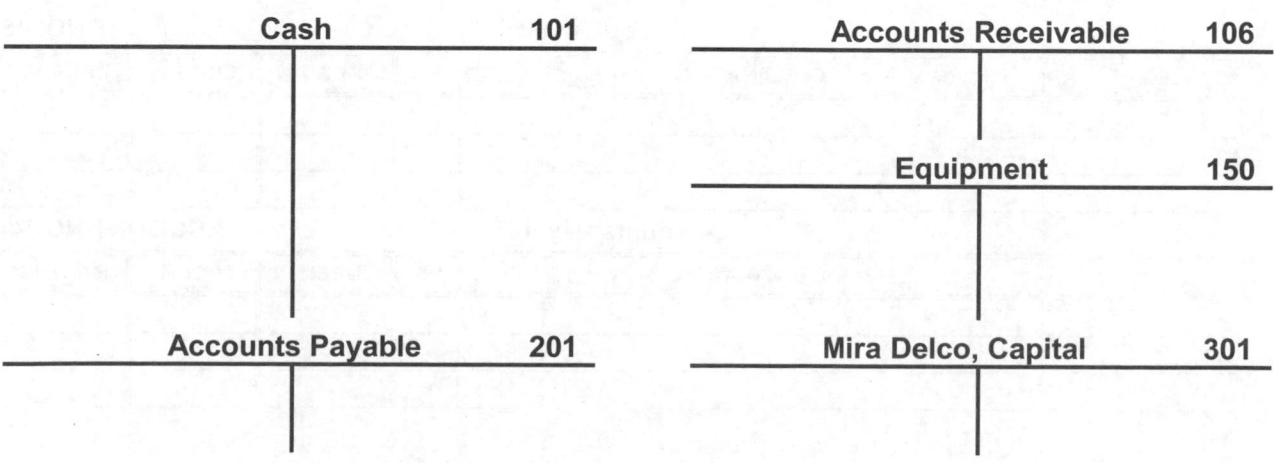

Cash 101	

Accounts Receivable 106	

Equipment 150	

Accounts Payable 201	

Mira Delco, Capital 301	

Mira Delco, Withdrawals   302

Revenue   401

Expenses   501

Parts 1 and 3

Note: T-accounts may be used or the balance column format; both are provided for in Parts 1 and 3 of this exercise.

GENERAL LEDGER

Cash   ACCOUNT NO. 101

DATE	EXPLANATION	PR	DEBIT	CREDIT	BALANCE

Accounts Receivable   ACCOUNT NO. 106

DATE	EXPLANATION	PR	DEBIT	CREDIT	BALANCE

Equipment   ACCOUNT NO. 150

DATE	EXPLANATION	PR	DEBIT	CREDIT	BALANCE

Accounts Payable   ACCOUNT NO. 201

DATE	EXPLANATION	PR	DEBIT	CREDIT	BALANCE

Mira Delco, Capital   ACCOUNT NO. 301

DATE	EXPLANATION	PR	DEBIT	CREDIT	BALANCE

Mira Delco, Withdrawals   ACCOUNT NO. 302

DATE	EXPLANATION	PR	DEBIT	CREDIT	BALANCE

Revenue   ACCOUNT NO. 401

DATE	EXPLANATION	PR	DEBIT	CREDIT	BALANCE

Expenses   ACCOUNT NO. 501

DATE	EXPLANATION	PR	DEBIT	CREDIT	BALANCE

Part 2

GENERAL JOURNAL   Page _____

Date	Account Titles and Explanation	PR	Debit	Credit

GENERAL JOURNAL   Page ____

Date	Account Titles and Explanation	PR	Debit	Credit

Part 4

_____

Trial Balance

_____

Part 5

_____

Income Statement

Statement of Changes in Equity

Balance Sheet

Analysis component:

_____

_____

_____

_____

_____

_____

_____

_____

_____

_____

Account Number	Account Name	Account Number	Account Name
_____	Cash	_____	Aaron Paquette, Withdrawals
_____	Accounts Receivable	_____	Consulting Revenues
_____	Office Equipment	_____	Salaries Expense
_____	Accounts Payable	_____	Rent Expense
_____	Unearned Revenue	_____	Utilities Expense
_____	Aaron Paquette, Capital		

GENERAL JOURNAL   Page ____

Date	Account Titles and Explanation	PR	Debit	Credit

Part 2

	Cash	101		Accounts Receivable	115
Bal.	15,000		Bal.	3,800	

				Office Equipment	160
			Bal.	22,500	

Accounts Payable		210
	8,000	Bal.

Unearned Revenue		215
	2,600	Bal.

Aaron Paquette, Capital		310
	9,500	Bal.

Aaron Paquette, Withdrawals		320
Bal.	2,000	

Consulting Revenues		410
	41,700	Bal.

Salaries Expense		510
Bal.	10,000	

Rent Expense		520
Bal.	7,500	

Utilities Expense		530
Bal.	1,000	

Part 3

Trial Balance

Part 4

Income Statement

Part 5

Statement of Changes in Equity

Part 6

Balance Sheet

Analysis component:

_____
_____
_____
_____
_____
_____
_____
_____
_____
_____
_____
_____
_____
_____
_____
_____
_____
_____

Exercise 2-7

GENERAL JOURNAL   Page ____

Date	Account Titles and Explanation	PR	Debit	Credit
a.				
b.				
c.				

GENERAL JOURNAL   Page ____

Date	Account Titles and Explanation	PR	Debit	Credit
d.				
e.				
f.				
g.				

Exercise 2-8

GENERAL JOURNAL   Page ____

Date	Account Titles and Explanation	PR	Debit	Credit

GENERAL JOURNAL   Page ____

Date	Account Titles and Explanation	PR	Debit	Credit

Chapter 2   Exercise 2-9   *Name* _____

Exercise 2-9

GENERAL JOURNAL   Page ____

Date	Account Titles and Explanation	PR	Debit	Credit

Transactions not creating revenue and the reasons:

_____
_____
_____
_____
_____
_____
_____
_____
_____
_____
_____
_____
_____
_____
_____

GENERAL JOURNAL   Page ____

Date	Account Titles and Explanation	PR	Debit	Credit

Transactions not creating revenue and the reasons:

_____

_____

_____

_____

_____

_____

_____

_____

_____

_____

_____

_____

_____

_____

GENERAL LEDGER

Cash   ACCOUNT NO. 101

DATE	EXPLANATION	PR	DEBIT	CREDIT	BALANCE
2013					
Dec. 31	Beginning balance				850

Accounts Receivable   ACCOUNT NO. 106

DATE	EXPLANATION	PR	DEBIT	CREDIT	BALANCE
2013					
Dec. 31	Beginning balance				300

Equipment   ACCOUNT NO. 167

DATE	EXPLANATION	PR	DEBIT	CREDIT	BALANCE
2013					
Dec. 31	Beginning balance				1,500

Accounts Payable   ACCOUNT NO. 201

DATE	EXPLANATION	PR	DEBIT	CREDIT	BALANCE
2013					
Dec. 31	Beginning balance				325

Jay Walker, Capital   ACCOUNT NO. 301

DATE	EXPLANATION	PR	DEBIT	CREDIT	BALANCE
2013					
Dec. 31	Beginning balance				2,325

Jay Walker, Withdrawals   ACCOUNT NO. 302

DATE	EXPLANATION	PR	DEBIT	CREDIT	BALANCE
2013					
Dec. 31	Beginning balance				300

Fees Earned   ACCOUNT NO. 401

DATE	EXPLANATION	PR	DEBIT	CREDIT	BALANCE
2013					
Dec. 31	Beginning balance				1,800

Salaries Expense   ACCOUNT NO. 622

DATE	EXPLANATION	PR	DEBIT	CREDIT	BALANCE
2013					
Dec. 31	Beginning balance				1,500

Analysis component:

_____
_____
_____
_____
_____
_____
_____
_____
_____
_____
_____
_____

GENERAL JOURNAL

Date	Account Titles and Explanation	PR	Debit	Credit

Cash   ACCOUNT NO. 101

DATE	EXPLANATION	PR	DEBIT	CREDIT	BALANCE

Office Supplies   ACCOUNT NO. 124

DATE	EXPLANATION	PR	DEBIT	CREDIT	BALANCE

Prepaid Rent   ACCOUNT NO. 131

DATE	EXPLANATION	PR	DEBIT	CREDIT	BALANCE

Photography Equipment   ACCOUNT NO. 167

DATE	EXPLANATION	PR	DEBIT	CREDIT	BALANCE

Joseph Eetok, Capital   ACCOUNT NO. 301

DATE	EXPLANATION	PR	DEBIT	CREDIT	BALANCE

Photography Fees Earned   ACCOUNT NO. 401

DATE	EXPLANATION	PR	DEBIT	CREDIT	BALANCE

Utilities Expense   ACCOUNT NO. 690

DATE	EXPLANATION	PR	DEBIT	CREDIT	BALANCE

Trial Balance

	Debit	Credit

Analysis component:

_____
_____
_____
_____
_____
_____
_____
_____
_____
_____

Cash	101		Office Supplies	124

Prepaid Rent	131		Photography Equipment	167

			Photography Fees Earned	401

Joseph Eetok, Capital	301		Utilities Expense	690

Trial Balance

	Debit	Credit

Analysis component:

_____
_____
_____
_____
_____
_____
_____

Income Statement

Statement of Changes in Equity

Balance Sheet

Analysis component:

_____

_____

_____

_____

_____

_____

_____

Income Statement

Statement of Changes in Equity

Balance Sheet

Income Statement

Statement of Changes in Equity

Balance Sheet

	Description	(1) Difference Between Debit and Credit Column	(2) Column With the Larger Total	(3) Identify Account(s) Incorrectly Stated	(4) Amount That Account(s) is Overstated or Understated
a.	A $2,400 debit to Rent Expense was posted as a $1,590 debit.	$810	Credit	Rent Expense	Rent Expense is understated by $810
b.	A $42,000 debit to Machinery was posted as a debit to Accounts Payable.				
c.	A $4,950 credit to Services Revenue was posted as a $495 credit.				
d.	A $1,440 debit to Store Supplies was not posted at all.				
e.	A $2,250 debit to Prepaid Insurance was posted as a debit to Insurance Expense.				
f.	A $4,050 credit to Cash was posted twice as two credits to the Cash account.				
g.	A $9,900 debit to the owner's withdrawals account was debited to the owner's capital account.				

Exercise 2-19

a. _____

_____

b. _____

_____

c. _____

_____

d. _____

_____

e. _____

_____

Case A: _____

_____

_____

_____

_____

_____

_____

_____

_____

_____

Case B: _____

_____

_____

_____

_____

_____

_____

_____

_____

Case C: _____

_____

_____

_____

_____

_____

_____

_____

_____

_____

_____

Parts 1 and 2

Cash

(a) 100,000	80,000 (b)
(g) 16,000	3,200 (f)
(n) 1,900	1,800 (h)
	4,600 (J)
	9,300 (K)
	3,200 (m)
	3,200 (o)

Land

(b) 115,000	

Accounts Payable

	(J) 4,600

Long-Term Notes Payable

	12,000

Accounts Receivable

(L) 5,100	1,900 (n)

Joel Douglas, Capital

	(a) 100,000
	(d) 9,000

C   D

Office Supplies

(C) 4,600	

Joel Douglas, Withdrawals

	(o) 3,200

Automobiles

(d) 9,000	

Fees Earned

	(g) 16,000

Office Equipment

(a) 9,000	(K) 700
(e) 3,000	
(k) 10,000	

Wages Expense

(f) 3,200	
(m) 3,200	

Building

(b) 85,00	

Utilities Expense

(h) 1,800	

GENERAL JOURNAL

Date	Account Titles and Explanation	PR	Debit	Credit

Chapter 2   Problem 2-2A (concl'd.)   *Name* _____

GENERAL JOURNAL   Page ____

Date	Account Titles and Explanation	PR	Debit	Credit

Problem 2-3A

GENERAL JOURNAL   Page ____

March

Date	Account Titles and Explanation	PR	Debit	Credit
1	Cash	101	50,000	
	office equipment	163	12,000	
	Abe. factor. capital	301		62,000
1	Prepaid rent	131	9,000	
	Cash	101		9,000
3	office equipment	163	6,000	
	office supplies	124	1,200	
	Account payable	201		7,200
5	Cash	101	6,200	
	Accounting Fees earned	401		6,200
9	Account Receivable	106	4,000	
	Accounting fees earned	401		4,000
11	Account payable	201	7,200	
	cash	101		7,200
15	Prepaid insurance	128	3,000	
	Cash	101		3,000
20	Cash	101	1,500	
	Account Receivable	106		1,500
22	No entry			
23	Account receivable	106	2,850	
	Accounting fees earned	401		2,850
27	Abe factor withdrew	302	3,600	
	Cash	101		3,600
30	office supplies	124	650	
	Accounts payable	201		650
31	Utility Expense	690	860	
	Cash	101		860

GENERAL JOURNAL   Page ____

Date	Account Titles and Explanation	PR	Debit	Credit
22	No entry			
23	Account Receivable	106	2850	
	Accounting fees earned	401		2850
27	Abe factor withdraw	302	3,600	
	Cash	101		3,600
30	office supplies	124	650	
	Accounts payable	201		650
31	Uitiliy expense	696	860	
	Cash	101		860

Problem 2-4A   Parts 1 and 2

GENERAL LEDGER

Cash   ACCOUNT NO. 101

DATE	EXPLANATION	PR	DEBIT	CREDIT	BALANCE
1	Cash		50,000		50,000
1			12,000	9,000	41,000
5			62,000	9,000	47,000
11				7200	40,000
15				3000	37,000
20			1,500		38,500
27				3600	34,900
31				860	34,040

Accounts Receivable ACCOUNT NO. 106

DATE	EXPLANATION	PR	DEBIT	CREDIT	BALANCE
9			4000		4000
20				1,500	2500
23			2,850		5350

Office Supplies ACCOUNT NO. 124

DATE	EXPLANATION	PR	DEBIT	CREDIT	BALANCE
3			1,200		1200
30			650		1850

Prepaid Insurance ACCOUNT NO. 128

DATE	EXPLANATION	PR	DEBIT	CREDIT	BALANCE
15			3,000		3000

Prepaid Rent ACCOUNT NO. 131

DATE	EXPLANATION	PR	DEBIT	CREDIT	BALANCE
1			9,000		9000

Office Equipment ACCOUNT NO. 163

DATE	EXPLANATION	PR	DEBIT	CREDIT	BALANCE
1			12,000		12000
			6,000		18000

Accounts Payable ACCOUNT NO. 201

DATE	EXPLANATION	PR	DEBIT	CREDIT	BALANCE
3				7,200	7,200
11			7,200		0
30				650	650

Abe Factor, Capital ACCOUNT NO. 301

DATE	EXPLANATION	PR	DEBIT	CREDIT	BALANCE
1				62,000	62,000

Abe Factor, Withdrawals ACCOUNT NO. 302

DATE	EXPLANATION	PR	DEBIT	CREDIT	BALANCE
27			3,600		3,600

 Name Sabreen

Accounting Fees Earned ACCOUNT NO. 40

DATE	EXPLANATION	PR	DEBIT	CREDIT	BALANCE
5				62,000	62,000
9				4000	10,200
23				2850	13,050

Utilities Expense ACCOUNT NO. 690

DATE	EXPLANATION	PR	DEBIT	CREDIT	BALANCE
31			860		860

Part 3

Trial Balance

	Debit	Credit
Cash	34040	
Account Receivable	5350	
Office Supplies	1850	
Prepaid Insurance	3000	
Prepaid Rent	9000	
Office Equipment	18000	
Account Payable		650
Capital		62,000
Withdrawals	3600	
Accounting Fees Earned		13050
Utilities Expense	860	
Total	$75,700	$75,700

Income Statement

	Debit	Credit
Revenues		
Accounting Fees Earned	13,050	
Operating expense		
Utilities Expense	860	
Net income		
Total	$12,190	

Statement of Changes in Equity

Abe Factor capital		
Add: Investments by owner	62,000	
Net income	12,190	74,190
Total		74,190
Less: Withdrawals by owner		3600
Abe Factor capital		
Total		$70,590

Balance Sheet

Assets		Liabilities	
Cash	$34,040	Account payable	650
AR			
OS			
Prepaid Insurance			
Prepaid rent			
office		Equity	
Total assets	71,240	Abe Factor capital	70,590
		Total liabilities and equity	71,240

GENERAL JOURNAL   Page ____

Date	Account Titles and Explanation	PR	Debit	Credit

GENERAL JOURNAL   Page ____

Date	Account Titles and Explanation	PR	Debit	Credit

Parts 2 and 3

GENERAL LEDGER

Cash   ACCOUNT NO. 101

DATE	EXPLANATION	PR	DEBIT	CREDIT	BALANCE

Accounts Receivable   ACCOUNT NO. 106

DATE	EXPLANATION	PR	DEBIT	CREDIT	BALANCE

Office Supplies   ACCOUNT NO. 124

DATE	EXPLANATION	PR	DEBIT	CREDIT	BALANCE

Prepaid Insurance   ACCOUNT NO. 128

DATE	EXPLANATION	PR	DEBIT	CREDIT	BALANCE

Prepaid Rent   ACCOUNT NO. 131

DATE	EXPLANATION	PR	DEBIT	CREDIT	BALANCE

Office Equipment   ACCOUNT NO. 163

DATE	EXPLANATION	PR	DEBIT	CREDIT	BALANCE

Accounts Payable   ACCOUNT NO. 201

DATE	EXPLANATION	PR	DEBIT	CREDIT	BALANCE

Jill Wahpoosywan, Capital   ACCOUNT NO. 301

DATE	EXPLANATION	PR	DEBIT	CREDIT	BALANCE

Jill Wahpoosywan, Withdrawals   ACCOUNT NO. 302

DATE	EXPLANATION	PR	DEBIT	CREDIT	BALANCE

Services Revenue   ACCOUNT NO. 403

DATE	EXPLANATION	PR	DEBIT	CREDIT	BALANCE

Wages Expense   ACCOUNT NO. 623

DATE	EXPLANATION	PR	DEBIT	CREDIT	BALANCE

Utilities Expense   ACCOUNT NO. 690

DATE	EXPLANATION	PR	DEBIT	CREDIT	BALANCE

Part 4

Trial Balance

Analysis component:

_____

_____

_____

_____

_____

_____

_____

_____

_____

_____

Income Statement

Statement of Changes in Equity

Balance Sheet

Income Statement

Statement of Changes in Equity

Balance Sheet

Analysis component: GENERAL JOURNAL   Page____

Date	Account Titles and Explanation	PR	Debit	Credit

Problem 2-9A

GENERAL JOURNAL   Page____

Date	Account Titles and Explanation	PR	Debit	Credit

GENERAL JOURNAL

Page____

Date	Account Titles and Explanation	PR	Debit	Credit

GENERAL JOURNAL   Page____

Date	Account Titles and Explanation	PR	Debit	Credit

Parts 2 and 3

GENERAL LEDGER

Cash   ACCOUNT NO. 101

DATE	EXPLANATION	PR	DEBIT	CREDIT	BALANCE
2014					
Jun. 30	Beginning balance				26,000

Accounts Receivable   ACCOUNT NO. 106

DATE	EXPLANATION	PR	DEBIT	CREDIT	BALANCE
2014					
Jun. 30	Beginning balance				3,000

Prepaid Insurance   ACCOUNT NO. 128

DATE	EXPLANATION	PR	DEBIT	CREDIT	BALANCE
2014					
Jun. 30	Beginning balance				500

Office Equipment   ACCOUNT NO. 163

DATE	EXPLANATION	PR	DEBIT	CREDIT	BALANCE
2014					
Jun. 30	Beginning balance				1,700

Drafting Equipment   ACCOUNT NO. 167

DATE	EXPLANATION	PR	DEBIT	CREDIT	BALANCE
2014					
Jun. 30	Beginning balance				1,200

Building   ACCOUNT NO. 173

DATE	EXPLANATION	PR	DEBIT	CREDIT	BALANCE
2014					
Jun. 30	Beginning balance				42,000

Land   ACCOUNT NO. 183

DATE	EXPLANATION	PR	DEBIT	CREDIT	BALANCE
2014					
Jun. 30	Beginning balance				28,000

Accounts Payable   ACCOUNT NO. 201

DATE	EXPLANATION	PR	DEBIT	CREDIT	BALANCE
2014					
Jun. 30	Beginning balance				1,740

Long-Term Notes Payable   ACCOUNT NO. 251

DATE	EXPLANATION	PR	DEBIT	CREDIT	BALANCE
2014					
Jun. 30	Beginning balance				24,000

Bishr Binbutti, Capital   ACCOUNT NO. 301

DATE	EXPLANATION	PR	DEBIT	CREDIT	BALANCE
2014					
Jun. 30	Beginning balance				54,000

Bishr Binbutti, Withdrawals   ACCOUNT NO. 302

DATE	EXPLANATION	PR	DEBIT	CREDIT	BALANCE
2014					
Jun. 30	Beginning balance				1,000

Engineering Fees Earned   ACCOUNT NO. 401

DATE	EXPLANATION	PR	DEBIT	CREDIT	BALANCE
2014					
Jun. 30	Beginning balance				29,600

Wages Expense   ACCOUNT NO. 623

DATE	EXPLANATION	PR	DEBIT	CREDIT	BALANCE
2014					
Jun. 30	Beginning balance				4,000

Equipment Rental Expense   ACCOUNT NO. 645

DATE	EXPLANATION	PR	DEBIT	CREDIT	BALANCE
2014					
Jun. 30	Beginning balance				1,000

Advertising Expense   ACCOUNT NO. 655

DATE	EXPLANATION	PR	DEBIT	CREDIT	BALANCE
2014					
Jun. 30	Beginning balance				640

Repairs Expense   ACCOUNT NO. 684

DATE	EXPLANATION	PR	DEBIT	CREDIT	BALANCE
2014					
Jun. 30	Beginning balance				300

Parts 4

Trial Balance

Income Statement

Statement of Changes in Equity

Balance Sheet

GENERAL JOURNAL

Page____

Date	Account Titles and Explanation	PR	Debit	Credit

Parts 2 and 3

Cash		101
Bal.	6,000	

Supplies		126
Bal.	950	

Furniture		161
Bal.	8,000	

Accounts Payable		201
	1,500	Bal.

Unearned Teaching Revenue		233
	9,800	Bal.

Teaching Revenue		401
	46,000	Bal.

Ted Ng, Capital		301
	3,000	Bal.

Wages Expense		623
Bal.	26,350	

Rent Expense		640
Bal.	6,000	

Ted Ng, Withdrawals		302
Bal.	13,000	

Trial Balance

Part 5

Income Statement

Statement of Changes in Equity

Balance Sheet

Income Statement

Statement of Changes in Equity

Balance Sheet

Analysis component:

GENERAL JOURNAL

Page____

Date	Account Titles and Explanation	PR	Debit	Credit

Problem 2-13A

Trial Balance

	Debit	Credit

Calculations:

_____
_____
_____
_____
_____
_____
_____
_____

Parts 1 and 2

Cash		Land

	Accounts Payable

	Long-Term Notes Payable

Accounts Receivable		Trevor Peeters, Capital

Office Supplies		Trevor Peeters, Withdrawals

Automobiles		Fees Earned

Office Equipment		Salaries Expense

	Utilities Expense

Building

Name _____

GENERAL JOURNAL

Page ____

Date	Account Titles and Explanation	PR	Debit	Credit

GENERAL JOURNAL   Page ____

Date	Account Titles and Explanation	PR	Debit	Credit

Problem 2-3B

GENERAL JOURNAL   Page ____

Date	Account Titles and Explanation	PR	Debit	Credit

GENERAL JOURNAL

Page ____

Date	Account Titles and Explanation	PR	Debit	Credit

GENERAL LEDGER

Cash ACCOUNT NO. 101

DATE	EXPLANATION	PR	DEBIT	CREDIT	BALANCE

Accounts Receivable ACCOUNT NO. 106

DATE	EXPLANATION	PR	DEBIT	CREDIT	BALANCE

Office Supplies ACCOUNT NO. 124

DATE	EXPLANATION	PR	DEBIT	CREDIT	BALANCE

Prepaid Insurance ACCOUNT NO. 128

DATE	EXPLANATION	PR	DEBIT	CREDIT	BALANCE

Prepaid Rent ACCOUNT NO. 131

DATE	EXPLANATION	PR	DEBIT	CREDIT	BALANCE

Office Equipment ACCOUNT NO. 163

DATE	EXPLANATION	PR	DEBIT	CREDIT	BALANCE

Accounts Payable   ACCOUNT NO. 201

DATE	EXPLANATION	PR	DEBIT	CREDIT	BALANCE

Susan Hurley, Capital   ACCOUNT NO. 301

DATE	EXPLANATION	PR	DEBIT	CREDIT	BALANCE

Susan Hurley, Withdrawals   ACCOUNT NO. 302

DATE	EXPLANATION	PR	DEBIT	CREDIT	BALANCE

Accounting Fees Earned   ACCOUNT NO. 401

DATE	EXPLANATION	PR	DEBIT	CREDIT	BALANCE

Professional Development Expense   ACCOUNT NO. 680

DATE	EXPLANATION	PR	DEBIT	CREDIT	BALANCE

Utilities Expense   ACCOUNT NO. 690

DATE	EXPLANATION	PR	DEBIT	CREDIT	BALANCE

Part 3

Trial Balance

Income Statement

Statement of Changes in Equity

Balance Sheet

GENERAL JOURNAL

Page____

Date	Account Titles and Explanation	PR	Debit	Credit

GENERAL JOURNAL   Page____

Date	Account Titles and Explanation	PR	Debit	Credit

Parts 2 and 3

GENERAL LEDGER

Cash   ACCOUNT NO. 101

DATE	EXPLANATION	PR	DEBIT	CREDIT	BALANCE

Accounts Receivable   ACCOUNT NO. 106

DATE	EXPLANATION	PR	DEBIT	CREDIT	BALANCE

Office Supplies   ACCOUNT NO. 12

DATE	EXPLANATION	PR	DEBIT	CREDIT	BALANCE

Prepaid Insurance   ACCOUNT NO. 128

DATE	EXPLANATION	PR	DEBIT	CREDIT	BALANCE

Prepaid Rent   ACCOUNT NO. 131

DATE	EXPLANATION	PR	DEBIT	CREDIT	BALANCE

Office Equipment   ACCOUNT NO. 163

DATE	EXPLANATION	PR	DEBIT	CREDIT	BALANCE

Accounts Payable   ACCOUNT NO. 20

DATE	EXPLANATION	PR	DEBIT	CREDIT	BALANCE

Tait Unger Annand, Capital   ACCOUNT NO. 301

DATE	EXPLANATION	PR	DEBIT	CREDIT	BALANCE

Tait Unger, Withdrawals   ACCOUNT NO. 302

DATE	EXPLANATION	PR	DEBIT	CREDIT	BALANCE

Service Fees Earned **ACCOUNT NO. 401**

DATE	EXPLANATION	PR	DEBIT	CREDIT	BALANCE

Wages Expense **ACCOUNT NO. 680**

DATE	EXPLANATION	PR	DEBIT	CREDIT	BALANCE

Utilities Expense **ACCOUNT NO. 690**

DATE	EXPLANATION	PR	DEBIT	CREDIT	BALANCE

Part 4

_____

Trial Balance

Analysis component:

_____
_____
_____
_____
_____
_____

Income Statement

Statement of Changes in Equity

Balance Sheet

Income Statement

Statement of Changes in Equity

Balance Sheet

Analysis Component:

GENERAL JOURNAL   Page ____

Date	Account Titles and Explanation	PR	Debit	Credit

Problem 2-9B   Part 1

GENERAL JOURNAL   Page ____

Date	Account Titles and Explanation	PR	Debit	Credit

GENERAL JOURNAL

Page ____

Date	Account Titles and Explanation	PR	Debit	Credit

Parts 2 and 3

GENERAL LEDGER

Cash   ACCOUNT NO. 101

DATE	EXPLANATION	PR	DEBIT	CREDIT	BALANCE
2014					
Jun. 30	Beginning balance				75,000

Accounts Receivable   ACCOUNT NO. 106

DATE	EXPLANATION	PR	DEBIT	CREDIT	BALANCE
2014					
Jun. 30	Beginning balance				950

Prepaid Insurance   ACCOUNT NO. 128

DATE	EXPLANATION	PR	DEBIT	CREDIT	BALANCE
2014					
Jun. 30	Beginning balance				275

Trucks   ACCOUNT NO. 153

DATE	EXPLANATION	PR	DEBIT	CREDIT	BALANCE
2014					
Jun. 30	Beginning balance				20,800

Office Equipment   ACCOUNT NO. 163

DATE	EXPLANATION	PR	DEBIT	CREDIT	BALANCE
2014					
Jun. 30	Beginning balance				1,200

Building   ACCOUNT NO. 173

DATE	EXPLANATION	PR	DEBIT	CREDIT	BALANCE
2014					
Jun. 30	Beginning balance				0

Land   ACCOUNT NO. 183

DATE	EXPLANATION	PR	DEBIT	CREDIT	BALANCE
2014					
Jun. 30	Beginning balance				0

Accounts Payable   ACCOUNT NO. 201

DATE	EXPLANATION	PR	DEBIT	CREDIT	BALANCE
2014					
Jun. 30	Beginning balance				725

Unearned Fees   ACCOUNT NO. 233

DATE	EXPLANATION	PR	DEBIT	CREDIT	BALANCE
2014					
Jun. 30	Beginning balance				0

Long-Term Notes Payable   ACCOUNT NO. 251

DATE	EXPLANATION	PR	DEBIT	CREDIT	BALANCE
2014					
Jun. 30	Beginning balance				7,000

Brett Wilson, Capital   ACCOUNT NO. 301

DATE	EXPLANATION	PR	DEBIT	CREDIT	BALANCE
2014					
Jun. 30	Beginning balance				83,825

Brett Wilson, Withdrawals   ACCOUNT NO. 302

DATE	EXPLANATION	PR	DEBIT	CREDIT	BALANCE
2014					
Jun. 30	Beginning balance				600

Fees Earned   ACCOUNT NO. 401

DATE	EXPLANATION	PR	DEBIT	CREDIT	BALANCE
2014					
Jun. 30	Beginning balance				8,400

Wages Expense   ACCOUNT NO. 623

DATE	EXPLANATION	PR	DEBIT	CREDIT	BALANCE
2014					
Jun. 30	Beginning balance				780

Truck Rental Expense   ACCOUNT NO. 645

DATE	EXPLANATION	PR	DEBIT	CREDIT	BALANCE
2014					
Jun. 30	Beginning balance				230

Advertising Expense   ACCOUNT NO. 655

DATE	EXPLANATION	PR	DEBIT	CREDIT	BALANCE
2014					
Jun. 30	Beginning balance				75

Repairs Expense   ACCOUNT NO. 684

DATE	EXPLANATION	PR	DEBIT	CREDIT	BALANCE
2014					
Jun. 30	Beginning balance				40

Part 4

Trial Balance

Income Statement

Statement of Changes in Equity

Balance Sheet

GENERAL JOURNAL   Page____

Date	Account Titles and Explanation	PR	Debit	Credit

Cash		101
Bal.	26,000	

Office Supplies		124
Bal.	900	

Office Equipment		163
Bal.	36,000	

Accounts Payable		201
	43,000	Bal.

Travel Revenue		401
	34,000	Bal.

Notes Payable		205
	20,000	Bal.

Wages Expense		623
Bal.	38,000	

Ike Petrov, Capital		301
	8,000	Bal.

Interest Expense		633
Bal.	100	

Ike Petrov, Withdrawals		302
Bal.	4,000	

Part 4

Trial Balance

Income Statement

Statement of Changes in Equity

Balance Sheet

Analysis component:

_____

_____

_____

_____

_____

_____

_____

_____

_____

Problem 2-12B

Income Statement

Statement of Changes in Equity

Balance Sheet

Trial Balance

Calculations:

Parts 2 and 6: October/November Transactions

GENERAL JOURNAL

Date	Account Titles and Explanation	PR	Debit	Credit

Echo Systems (Cont'd.)

Date	Account Titles and Explanation	PR	Debit	Credit

Date	Account Titles and Explanation	PR	Debit	Credit

Cash   ACCOUNT NO. 101

DATE	EXPLANATION	PR	DEBIT	CREDIT	BALANCE

Accounts Receivable   ACCOUNT NO. 106

DATE	EXPLANATION	PR	DEBIT	CREDIT	BALANCE

Computer Supplies   ACCOUNT NO. 126

DATE	EXPLANATION	PR	DEBIT	CREDIT	BALANCE

Prepaid Insurance   ACCOUNT NO. 128

DATE	EXPLANATION	PR	DEBIT	CREDIT	BALANCE

Prepaid Rent   ACCOUNT NO. 131

DATE	EXPLANATION	PR	DEBIT	CREDIT	BALANCE

Office Equipment   ACCOUNT NO. 163

DATE	EXPLANATION	PR	DEBIT	CREDIT	BALANCE

Computer Equipment   ACCOUNT NO. 167

DATE	EXPLANATION	PR	DEBIT	CREDIT	BALANCE

Accounts Payable   ACCOUNT NO. 2

DATE	EXPLANATION	PR	DEBIT	CREDIT	BALANCE

Mary Graham, Capital   ACCOUNT NO. 301

DATE	EXPLANATION	PR	DEBIT	CREDIT	BALANCE

Mary Graham, Withdrawals   ACCOUNT NO. 302

DATE	EXPLANATION	PR	DEBIT	CREDIT	BALANCE

Computer Services Revenue — ACCOUNT NO. 403

DATE	EXPLANATION	PR	DEBIT	CREDIT	BALANCE

Wages Expense — ACCOUNT NO. 623

DATE	EXPLANATION	PR	DEBIT	CREDIT	BALANCE

Advertising Expense — ACCOUNT NO. 655

DATE	EXPLANATION	PR	DEBIT	CREDIT	BALANCE

Mileage Expense — ACCOUNT NO. 676

DATE	EXPLANATION	PR	DEBIT	CREDIT	BALANCE

Repairs Expense, Computer — ACCOUNT NO. 684

DATE	EXPLANATION	PR	DEBIT	CREDIT	BALANCE

Charitable Donations Expense — ACCOUNT NO. 699

DATE	EXPLANATION	PR	DEBIT	CREDIT	BALANCE

Part 4

ECHO SYSTMES
Trial Balance
October 31, 2014

	Debit	Credit

Part 5

ECHO SYSTEMS
Income Statement
Month Ended October 31, 2014

ECHO SYSTEMS
Statement of Changes in Equity
Month Ended October 31, 2014

ECHO SYSTEMS
Balance Sheet
October 31, 2014

Part 8

ECHO SYSTEMS
Trial Balance
November 30, 2014

	Debit	Credit

Part 9

ECHO SYSTEMS
Income Statement
For Two Months Ended November 30, 2014

ECHO SYSTEMS
Statement of Changes in Equity
For Two Months Ended November 30, 2014

ECHO SYSTEMS
Balance Sheet
November 30, 2014

1. _____
_____
_____

2. _____
_____
_____

3. _____
_____
_____

4. _____
_____
_____

Quick Study 3-2

Cash Basis: _____
_____
_____
_____

Accrual Basis: _____
_____
_____
_____
_____

Quick Study 3-3

GENERAL JOURNAL   Page____

Date	Account Titles and Explanation	PR	Debit	Credit
a.				
b.				
c.				
d.				

GENERAL JOURNAL   Page____

Date	Account Titles and Explanation	PR	Debit	Credit

Quick Study 3-5

GENERAL JOURNAL   Page____

Date	Account Titles and Explanation	PR	Debit	Credit

GENERAL JOURNAL   Page____

Date	Account Titles and Explanation	PR	Debit	Credit

Quick Study 3-7

GENERAL JOURNAL   Page____

Date	Account Titles and Explanation	PR	Debit	Credit

Quick Study 3-8

	Debit	Credit	
a.	_____	_____	Accrual of unpaid and unrecorded advertising that was used by Stark Company.
b.	_____	_____	Adjustment of Unearned Services Revenue to recognize earned revenue.
c.	_____	_____	Recorded revenue for work completed this accounting period; the cash will be received in the next period.
d.	_____	_____	The cost of Equipment was matched to the time periods benefited.
e.	_____	_____	Adjustment of Prepaid Advertising to recognize the portion used.

	Dr./Cr.	Account Titles	Statement
(a)	Debit		
	Credit		
(b)	Debit		
	Credit		
(c)	Debit		
	Credit		
(d)	Debit		
	Credit		
(e)	Debit		
	Credit		

Quick Study 3-10

		If adjustment is not recorded:			
	Type of Adjustment	Net income will be overstated, understated, or no effect	Assets will be overstated, understated, or no effect	Liabilities will be overstated, understated, or no effect	Equity will be overstated, understated, or no effect
a.	Prepaid Expenses				
b.	Depreciation				
c.	Unearned Revenues				
d.	Accrued Expenses				
e.	Accrued Revenues				

Quick Study 3-11

GENERAL JOURNAL   Page____

Date	Account Titles and Explanation	PR	Debit	Credit

GENERAL JOURNAL   Page____

Date	Account Titles and Explanation	PR	Debit	Credit

*Quick Study 3-13

GENERAL JOURNAL   Page____

Date	Account Titles and Explanation	PR	Debit	Credit

GENERAL JOURNAL   Page____

Date	Account Titles and Explanation	PR	Debit	Credit
a.				
b.				
c.				
d.				

Name _____

1. _____   7. _____
2. _____   8. _____
3. _____   9. _____
4. _____   10. _____
5. _____   11. _____
6. _____   12. _____

Exercise 3-2

GENERAL JOURNAL   Page____

Date	Account Titles and Explanation	PR	Debit	Credit
a.				
b.				
c.				
d.				
e.				
f.				
g.				

Name _____

GENERAL JOURNAL

Page____

Date	Account Titles and Explanation	PR	Debit	Credit
a.				
b.				
c.				
d.				
e.				
f.				
g.				

GENERAL JOURNAL   Page____

Date	Account Titles and Explanation	PR	Debit	Credit
a.				
b.				
c.				
d.				
e.				
f.				
g.				

GENERAL JOURNAL   Page____

Date	Account Titles and Explanation	PR	Debit	Credit
a.				
b.				
c.				

Exercise 3-6

GENERAL JOURNAL   Page____

Date	Account Titles and Explanation	PR	Debit	Credit
a.				
b.				
c.				
d.				
e.				

a. _____
_____
_____

b. _____
_____
_____

c. _____
_____
_____

d. _____
_____
_____

Exercise 3-8

Adjusting Entry:

GENERAL JOURNAL   Page____

Date		Account Titles and Explanation	PR	Debit	Credit

Payday Entry:

GENERAL JOURNAL   Page____

Date		Account Titles and Explanation	PR	Debit	Credit

Chapter 3   Exercise 3-9   *Name* _____

(a)
Adjusting Entry:

GENERAL JOURNAL   Page____

Date	Account Titles and Explanation	PR	Debit	Credit

Journal Entry (Next Period):

GENERAL JOURNAL   Page____

Date	Account Titles and Explanation	PR	Debit	Credit

(b)
Adjusting Entry:

GENERAL JOURNAL   Page____

Date	Account Titles and Explanation	PR	Debit	Credit

Journal Entry (Next Period):

GENERAL JOURNAL   Page____

Date	Account Titles and Explanation	PR	Debit	Credit

(c)
Adjusting Entry:

GENERAL JOURNAL   Page____

Date	Account Titles and Explanation	PR	Debit	Credit

Journal Entry (Next Period):

GENERAL JOURNAL   Page____

Date	Account Titles and Explanation	PR	Debit	Credit

Exercise 3-10

GENERAL JOURNAL   Page____

Date	Account Titles and Explanation	PR	Debit	Credit

GENERAL JOURNAL   Page____

Date	Account Titles and Explanation	PR	Debit	Credit

Analysis component:

_____

_____

_____

_____

_____

ACCOUNT	UNADJUSTED TRIAL BALANCE		ADJUSTMENTS		ADJUSTED TRIAL BALANCE	
	Debit	Credit	Debit	Credit	Debit	Credit
Cash	$ 14,000					
Accounts receivable	32,000					
Prepaid insurance	16,800					
Equipment	102,000					
Accum. deprec., equipment		$ 23,000				
Accounts payable		19,000				
Abraham Nuna, capital		213,000				
Abraham Nuna, withdrawals	102,000					
Revenues		214,000				
Deprec. exp., equipment	-0-					
Salaries expense	187,700					
Insurance expense	14,500					
Totals	$469,000	$469,000				

Exercise 3-12

Income Statement

Statement of Changes in Equity

Balance Sheet

Analysis component:

*Exercise 3-13

GENERAL JOURNAL   Page____

Date		Account Titles and Explanation	PR	Debit	Credit
a.					
b.					

GENERAL JOURNAL   Page____

Date	Account Titles and Explanation	PR	Debit	Credit
c.				
d.				

Analysis component:

_____
_____
_____
_____
_____
_____

GENERAL JOURNAL   Page____

Date	Account Titles and Explanation	PR	Debit	Credit
a.				
b.				
c.				
d.				
e.				
f.				

Chapter 3   *Exercise 3-15   *Name* _____

a. Initial credit recorded in Unearned Fees account:

GENERAL JOURNAL   Page____

Date	Account Titles and Explanation	PR	Debit	Credit

b. Initial credit recorded in Fees Earned account:

GENERAL JOURNAL   Page____

Date	Account Titles and Explanation	PR	Debit	Credit

c.

GENERAL JOURNAL   Page____

Date	Account Titles and Explanation	PR	Debit	Credit
a.				
b.				
c.				
d.				

Analysis component:

_____

_____

_____

_____

Problem 3-2A

GENERAL JOURNAL   Page____

Date	Account Titles and Explanation	PR	Debit	Credit
a.				
b.				
c.				

Analysis component:

_____
_____
_____
_____
_____
_____
_____
_____
_____

Problem 3-3A

GENERAL JOURNAL   Page____

Date	Account Titles and Explanation	PR	Debit	Credit
a.				
b.				
c.				
d.				

Analysis component:

_____
_____
_____
_____
_____
_____
_____
_____

Adjusting Entries: **GENERAL JOURNAL**   **Page____**

Date	Account Titles and Explanation	PR	Debit	Credit
a.				
b.				
c.				
d.				
e.				

Subsequent Entries: GENERAL JOURNAL Page____

Date	Account Titles and Explanation	PR	Debit	Credit
a.				
b.				
c.				
d.				
e.				

Adjusting Entries: GENERAL JOURNAL   Page____

Date	Account Titles and Explanation	PR	Debit	Credit
a.				
b.				
c.				
d.				

Subsequent Entries: GENERAL JOURNAL   Page____

Date	Account Titles and Explanation	PR	Debit	Credit
a.				
b.				
c.				
d.				

GENERAL JOURNAL   Page____

Date	Account Titles and Explanation	PR	Debit	Credit
a.				
b.				
c.				
d.				
e.				
f.				
g.				
h.				

Part 2: *See next page for Part 2 working paper.*

Part 3: _____

_____

_____

Part 4: _____

_____

_____

Part 2

ACCOUNT	UNADJUSTED TRIAL BALANCE		ADJUSTMENTS		ADJUSTED TRIAL BALANCE	
	Debit	Credit	Debit	Credit	Debit	Credit
Cash	$ 18,000					
Accounts receivable	-0-					
Teaching supplies	6,500					
Prepaid insurance	1,400					
Prepaid rent	7,200					
Professional library	60,000					
Accum. deprec., library		18,000				
Equipment	96,000					
Accum. deprec., equipment		32,000				
Accounts payable		2,500				
Salaries payable		-0-				
Unearned extension fees		6,300				
Karoo Ashevak, capital		229,000				
Karoo Ashevak, withdrwls	92,000					
Tuition fees earned		196,000				
Extension fees earned		72,500				
Deprec. exp., equipment	-0-					
Deprec. exp., library	-0-					
Salaries expense	206,000					
Insurance expense	-0-					
Rent expense	44,000					
Teaching supplies expense	-0-					
Advertising expense	14,000					
Utilities expense	11,200					
Totals	$556,300	$556,300				

Problem 3-7A

GENERAL JOURNAL   Page____

Date		Account Titles and Explanation	PR	Debit	Credit
a.					
b.					

GENERAL JOURNAL   Page____

Date	Account Titles and Explanation	PR	Debit	Credit
c.				
d.				
e.				
f.				
g.				
h.				
i.				
j.				

Part 1   **GENERAL JOURNAL**   Page____

Date	Account Titles and Explanation	PR	Debit	Credit
a.				
b.				
c.				
d.				
e.				
f.				

Part 2   GENERAL JOURNAL   Page____

Date	Account Titles and Explanation	PR	Debit	Credit

Problem 3-9A

GENERAL JOURNAL   Page____

Date	Account Titles and Explanation	PR	Debit	Credit
a.				
b.				
c.				
d.				

GENERAL JOURNAL

Page____

Date	Account Titles and Explanation	PR	Debit	Credit
e.				
f.				
g.				
h.				
i.				

Problem 3-10A   Parts 1 and 2

GENERAL LEDGER

Cash   ACCOUNT NO. 101

DATE	EXPLANATION	PR	DEBIT	CREDIT	BALANCE
2014					
Oct. 31	Balance				26,000

Accounts Receivable   ACCOUNT NO. 106

DATE	EXPLANATION	PR	DEBIT	CREDIT	BALANCE
2014					
Oct. 31	Balance				61,000

Interest Receivable   ACCOUNT NO. 109

DATE	EXPLANATION	PR	DEBIT	CREDIT	BALANCE
2014					

Notes Receivable   ACCOUNT NO. 111

DATE	EXPLANATION	PR	DEBIT	CREDIT	BALANCE
2014					
Oct. 31	Balance				50,000

Supplies   ACCOUNT NO. 126

DATE	EXPLANATION	PR	DEBIT	CREDIT	BALANCE
2014					
Oct. 31	Balance				5,300

Prepaid Insurance   ACCOUNT NO. 128

DATE	EXPLANATION	PR	DEBIT	CREDIT	BALANCE
2014					
Oct. 31	Balance				3,400

Prepaid Rent   ACCOUNT NO. 131

DATE	EXPLANATION	PR	DEBIT	CREDIT	BALANCE
2014					
Oct. 31	Balance				27,000

Office Furniture   ACCOUNT NO. 161

DATE	EXPLANATION	PR	DEBIT	CREDIT	BALANCE
2014					
Oct. 31	Balance				84,000

Accumulated Depreciation, Office Furniture   ACCOUNT NO. 162

DATE	EXPLANATION	PR	DEBIT	CREDIT	BALANCE
2014					
Oct. 31	Balance				28,000

Accounts Payable
ACCOUNT NO. 201

DATE	EXPLANATION	PR	DEBIT	CREDIT	BALANCE
2014					
Oct. 31	Balance				18,000

Wages Payable
ACCOUNT NO. 210

DATE	EXPLANATION	PR	DEBIT	CREDIT	BALANCE
2014					

Unearned Consulting Fees
ACCOUNT NO. 233

DATE	EXPLANATION	PR	DEBIT	CREDIT	BALANCE
2014					
Oct. 31	Balance				26,000

Jeff Moore, Capital
ACCOUNT NO. 301

DATE	EXPLANATION	PR	DEBIT	CREDIT	BALANCE
2014					
Oct. 31	Balance				223,000

Jeff Moore, Withdrawals
ACCOUNT NO. 302

DATE	EXPLANATION	PR	DEBIT	CREDIT	BALANCE
2014					
Oct. 31	Balance				28,000

Consulting Fees Earned
ACCOUNT NO. 401

DATE	EXPLANATION	PR	DEBIT	CREDIT	BALANCE
2014					
Oct. 31	Balance				232,020

Interest Revenue   ACCOUNT NO. 409

DATE	EXPLANATION	PR	DEBIT	CREDIT	BALANCE
2014					
Oct. 31	Balance				480

Depreciation Expense, Office Furniture   ACCOUNT NO. 601

DATE	EXPLANATION	PR	DEBIT	CREDIT	BALANCE
2014					

Wages Expense   ACCOUNT NO. 622

DATE	EXPLANATION	PR	DEBIT	CREDIT	BALANCE
2014					
Oct. 31	Balance				192,000

Insurance Expense   ACCOUNT NO. 637

DATE	EXPLANATION	PR	DEBIT	CREDIT	BALANCE
2014					

Rent Expense   ACCOUNT NO. 640

DATE	EXPLANATION	PR	DEBIT	CREDIT	BALANCE
2014					
Oct. 31	Balance				44,000

Supplies Expense   ACCOUNT NO. 650

DATE	EXPLANATION	PR	DEBIT	CREDIT	BALANCE
2014					
Oct. 31	Balance				6,800

Adjusted Trial Balance

Part 4

Income Statement

Statement of Changes in Equity

Balance Sheet

Analysis component:

_____

_____

_____

_____

_____

_____

GENERAL JOURNAL   Page____

Date	Account Titles and Explanation	PR	Debit	Credit
a.				
b.				
c.				
d.				
e.				
f.				
g.				

Chapter 3   Problem 3-12A   Part 1   *Name* _____

ACCOUNT	UNADJUSTED TRIAL BALANCE		ADJUSTMENTS		ADJUSTED TRIAL BALANCE	
	Debit	Credit	Debit	Credit	Debit	Credit
Cash	$ 6,000					
Accounts receivable	11,200					
Repair supplies	2,200					
Prepaid rent	14,000					
Office furniture	26,000					
Accounts payable		$ 8,000				
Notes payable		21,600				
Eli Arrow, capital		67,758				
Eli Arrow, withdrawals	5,000					
Hospitality revenues		128,000				
Salaries expense	144,000					
Wages expense	16,958					
Totals	$225,358	$225,358				

Part 2

Income Statement

Statement of Changes in Equity

Balance Sheet

Analysis component:

_____
_____
_____
_____
_____
_____
_____
_____

Part a.

Income Statement

Part b.

Statement of Changes in Equity

Part c.
_____

Balance Sheet

Analysis component:

_____
_____
_____
_____
_____
_____
_____
_____
_____

GENERAL JOURNAL

Page____

Date	Account Titles and Explanation	PR	Debit	Credit

Parts 2, 3 and 5

Cash	101		Prepaid Rent	131

Office Furniture	161		Accum. Deprec., Office Furn.	162

Accounts Payable	201		Unearned Revenue	233

Delanie Tugut, Capital	301		Delanie Tugut, Withdrawals	302

Revenue	401		Deprec. Exp., Office Furniture	602

Wages Expense	623		Rent Expense	640

Telephone Expense	688		Hotel Expenses	696

Part 4

Trial Balance

	Debit	Credit

Part 5 – Adjusting entries

GENERAL JOURNAL   Page____

Date	Account Titles and Explanation	PR	Debit	Credit

Part 6

Trial Balance

	Debit	Credit

Part 7

Income Statement

Part 7 (concl'd.)

Statement of Changes in Equity

Balance Sheet

Analysis component:

_____
_____
_____
_____
_____
_____
_____
_____

GENERAL JOURNAL

Page____

Date	Account Titles and Explanation	PR	Debit	Credit
a.				
b.				
c.				
d.				
e.				

Analysis component:

_____
_____
_____
_____
_____
_____
_____

ACCOUNT	UNADJUSTED TRIAL BALANCE		ADJUSTMENTS		ADJUSTED TRIAL BALANCE	
	Debit	Credit	Debit	Credit	Debit	Credit
Cash	$ 32,000					
Accounts receivable	63,000					
Prepaid rent	-0-					
Prepaid insurance	-0-					
Accounts payable		$ 16,000				
Unearned consulting fees		-0-				
Bruce Willis, capital		38,400				
Consulting fees earned		82,000				
Rent expense	38,990					
Insurance expense	2,410					
Totals	$136,400	$136,400				

*Problem 3-17A

Part 1 - Entries that initially recognize assets and liabilities:

GENERAL JOURNAL   Page____

Date	Account Titles and Explanation	PR	Debit	Credit

GENERAL JOURNAL   Page____

Date	Account Titles and Explanation	PR	Debit	Credit

Part 2 – Entries that initially recognize expenses and revenues:

GENERAL JOURNAL   Page____

Date	Account Titles and Explanation	PR	Debit	Credit

Part 2 (concluded)

GENERAL JOURNAL Page____

Date	Account Titles and Explanation	PR	Debit	Credit

Analysis component:

_____
_____
_____
_____
_____
_____
_____
_____
_____
_____
_____
_____
_____
_____

GENERAL JOURNAL   Page____

Date	Account Titles and Explanation	PR	Debit	Credit
a.				
b.				
c.				
d.				

Analysis component:

_____

_____

_____

_____

Problem 3-2B

GENERAL JOURNAL   Page____

Date	Account Titles and Explanation	PR	Debit	Credit
a.				
b.				
c.				

Analysis component:

_____
_____
_____
_____
_____
_____
_____
_____
_____

Problem 3-3B

GENERAL JOURNAL   Page____

Date	Account Titles and Explanation	PR	Debit	Credit
a.				
b.				
c.				
d.				

Analysis component:

_____
_____
_____
_____
_____
_____
_____
_____

Adjusting Entries: **GENERAL JOURNAL**   Page____

Date	Account Titles and Explanation	PR	Debit	Credit
a.				
b.				
c.				
d.				
e.				

Subsequent Entries: **GENERAL JOURNAL**   Page____

Date	Account Titles and Explanation	PR	Debit	Credit
a.				
b.				
c.				
d.				
e.				

Adjusting Entries: **GENERAL JOURNAL**   Page____

Date		Account Titles and Explanation	PR	Debit	Credit
a.					
b.					
c.					
d.					

Subsequent Entries: **GENERAL JOURNAL**   Page____

Date		Account Titles and Explanation	PR	Debit	Credit
a.					
b.					
c.					
d.					

GENERAL JOURNAL   Page____

Date	Account Titles and Explanation	PR	Debit	Credit
a.				
b.				
c.				
d.				
e.				
f.				
g.				
h.				

Part 2: *See next page for Part 2 working paper.*

Part 3: _____

_____

_____

Part 4: _____

_____

_____

Chapter 3   Problem 3-6B (concl'd.)   *Name* _____

Part 2

ACCOUNT	UNADJUSTED TRIAL BALANCE		ADJUSTMENTS		ADJUSTED TRIAL BALANCE	
	Debit	Credit	Debit	Credit	Debit	Credit
Cash	$ 25,000					
Accounts receivable	-0-					
Teaching supplies	107,200					
Prepaid insurance	36,000					
Prepaid rent	11,600					
Professional library	20,000					
Accum. deprec., library		3,000				
Equipment	141,400					
Accum. deprec., equipment		32,000				
Accounts payable		24,400				
Salaries payable		-0-				
Unearned extension fees		55,200				
Jay Fawcett, capital		62,000				
Jay Fawcett, withdrawals	40,000					
Tuition fees earned		285,000				
Extension fees earned		124,000				
Deprec. exp., equipment	-0-					
Deprec. exp., library	-0-					
Salaries expense	143,600					
Insurance expense	-0-					
Rent expense	-0-					
Teaching supplies expense	-0-					
Advertising expense	36,000					
Utilities expense	24,800					
Totals	$585,600	$585,600				

Problem 3-7B

Subsequent Entries: **GENERAL JOURNAL**   Page_____

Date	Account Titles and Explanation	PR	Debit	Credit
a.				
b.				

GENERAL JOURNAL

Page____

Date	Account Titles and Explanation	PR	Debit	Credit
c.				
d.				
e.				
f.				
g.				
h.				
i.				
j.				

Name _____

GENERAL JOURNAL

Page____

Date	Account Titles and Explanation	PR	Debit	Credit
a.				
b.				
c.				
d.				
e.				
f.				

Part 2   GENERAL JOURNAL   Page____

Date	Account Titles and Explanation	PR	Debit	Credit

Problem 3-9B

GENERAL JOURNAL   Page____

Date	Account Titles and Explanation	PR	Debit	Credit
a.				
b.				
c.				
d.				

GENERAL JOURNAL

Page____

Date	Account Titles and Explanation	PR	Debit	Credit
e.				
f.				
g.				
h.				
i.				

Analysis component:

_____

_____

_____

_____

_____

_____

_____

_____

Parts 1 and 2

Cash   ACCOUNT NO. 101

DATE	EXPLANATION	PR	DEBIT	CREDIT	BALANCE
2014					
Dec. 31	Balance				15,600

Accounts Receivable   ACCOUNT NO. 106

DATE	EXPLANATION	PR	DEBIT	CREDIT	BALANCE
2014					
Dec. 31	Balance				29,200

Supplies   ACCOUNT NO. 126

DATE	EXPLANATION	PR	DEBIT	CREDIT	BALANCE
2014					
Dec. 31	Balance				1,640

Prepaid Advertising   ACCOUNT NO. 128

DATE	EXPLANATION	PR	DEBIT	CREDIT	BALANCE
2014					
Dec. 31	Balance				1,280

Prepaid Rent   ACCOUNT NO. 131

DATE	EXPLANATION	PR	DEBIT	CREDIT	BALANCE
2014					
Dec. 31	Balance				17,880

Surveying Equipment   ACCOUNT NO. 167

DATE	EXPLANATION	PR	DEBIT	CREDIT	BALANCE
2014					
Dec. 31	Balance				58,000

Accum. Deprec. – Surveying Equipment   ACCOUNT NO. 168

DATE	EXPLANATION	PR	DEBIT	CREDIT	BALANCE
2014					
Dec. 31	Balance				7,348

Accounts Payable ACCOUNT NO. 201

DATE	EXPLANATION	PR	DEBIT	CREDIT	BALANCE
2014					
Dec. 31	Balance				13,800

Interest Payable ACCOUNT NO. 203

DATE	EXPLANATION	PR	DEBIT	CREDIT	BALANCE
2014					

Wages Payable ACCOUNT NO. 210

DATE	EXPLANATION	PR	DEBIT	CREDIT	BALANCE
2014					

Unearned Surveying Fees ACCOUNT NO. 233

DATE	EXPLANATION	PR	DEBIT	CREDIT	BALANCE
2014					
Dec. 31	Balance				14,80

Notes Payable ACCOUNT NO. 251

DATE	EXPLANATION	PR	DEBIT	CREDIT	BALANCE
2014					
Dec. 31	Balance				36,000

Ben Hallmark, Capital ACCOUNT NO. 301

DATE	EXPLANATION	PR	DEBIT	CREDIT	BALANCE
2014					
Dec. 31	Balance				28,652

Ben Hallmark, Withdrawals ACCOUNT NO. 302

DATE	EXPLANATION	PR	DEBIT	CREDIT	BALANCE
2014					
Dec. 31	Balance				24,300

Surveying Fees Earned   ACCOUNT NO. 401

DATE	EXPLANATION	PR	DEBIT	CREDIT	BALANCE
2014					
Dec. 31	Balance				170,948

Depreciation Expense, Surveying Equipment   ACCOUNT NO. 601

DATE	EXPLANATION	PR	DEBIT	CREDIT	BALANCE
2014					

Salaries Expense   ACCOUNT NO. 622

DATE	EXPLANATION	PR	DEBIT	CREDIT	BALANCE
2014					
Dec. 31	Balance				56,000

Wages Expense   ACCOUNT NO. 623

DATE	EXPLANATION	PR	DEBIT	CREDIT	BALANCE
2014					
Dec. 31	Balance				39,726

Interest Expense   ACCOUNT NO. 633

DATE	EXPLANATION	PR	DEBIT	CREDIT	BALANCE
2014					

Insurance Expense   ACCOUNT NO. 637

DATE	EXPLANATION	PR	DEBIT	CREDIT	BALANCE
2014					
Dec. 31	Balance				6,000

Rent Expense   ACCOUNT NO. 640

DATE	EXPLANATION	PR	DEBIT	CREDIT	BALANCE
2014					

Supplies Expense   ACCOUNT NO. 650

DATE	EXPLANATION	PR	DEBIT	CREDIT	BALANCE
2014					
Dec. 31	Balance				2,958

Advertising Expense   ACCOUNT NO. 655

DATE	EXPLANATION	PR	DEBIT	CREDIT	BALANCE
2014					

Gas and Oil Expense   ACCOUNT NO. 671

DATE	EXPLANATION	PR	DEBIT	CREDIT	BALANCE
2014					
Dec. 31	Balance				6,564

Repairs Expense   ACCOUNT NO. 684

DATE	EXPLANATION	PR	DEBIT	CREDIT	BALANCE
2014					
Dec. 31	Balance				12,400

Utilities Expense   ACCOUNT NO. 690

DATE	EXPLANATION	PR	DEBIT	CREDIT	BALANCE
2014					

Adjusted Trial Balance

Income Statement

Statement of Changes in Equity

Balance Sheet

Analysis component:

_____

_____

_____

_____

_____

_____

_____

_____

_____

_____

_____

GENERAL JOURNAL   Page____

Date	Account Titles and Explanation	PR	Debit	Credit
a.				
b.				
c.				
d.				
e.				
f.				
g.				

ACCOUNT	UNADJUSTED TRIAL BALANCE		ADJUSTMENTS		ADJUSTED TRIAL BALANCE	
	Debit	Credit	Debit	Credit	Debit	Credit
Cash	$ 112,000					
Accounts receivable	28,000					
Repair supplies	2,800					
Prepaid arena rental	182,000					
Skate equipment	428,000					
Accum. deprec., skate eq.		$ 164,000				
Accounts payable		5,400				
Unearned training fees		19,600				
Notes payable		160,000				
Ben Gibson, capital		451,400				
Ben Gibson, withdrawals	72,000					
Training fees earned		550,000				
Salaries expense	350,000					
Arena rental expense	168,000					
Other expenses	7,600					
Totals	$1,350,400	$1,350,400				

Part 2

Income Statement

Statement of Changes in Equity

Balance Sheet

Analysis component:

_____
_____
_____
_____
_____
_____

Income Statement

Statement of Changes in Equity

Balance Sheet

GENERAL JOURNAL

Date	Account Titles and Explanation	PR	Debit	Credit

Parts 2, 3, and 5

Cash	101
Bal. 6,400	

Repair Supplies	131
Bal. 3,000	

Accum. Deprec., Tools	162
	560 Bal.

Tools	161
Bal. 16,800	

Accounts Payable	201
	3,200 Bal.

Unearned Revenue	233
	700 Bal.

Melanie Thornhill, Capital	301
	Bal.

Melanie Thornhill, Withdrawals	302
Bal. -0-	

Revenue	401
	25,800 Bal.

Deprec. Exp., Tools	602
Bal. 560	

Wages Expense	623
Bal. 1,960	

Rent Expense	640
Bal. 8,000	

Repairs Supplies Expense	696
Bal. 2,700	

Part 4

Trial Balance

	Debit	Credit

Part 5 – Adjusting entries

GENERAL JOURNAL   Page_____

Date	Account Titles and Explanation	PR	Debit	Credit

Part 6

Trial Balance

	Debit	Credit

Part 7

Income Statement

Part 6 (concl'd.)

Statement of Changes in Equity

Balance Sheet

Analysis component:

_____

_____

_____

_____

_____

_____

_____

GENERAL JOURNAL   Page____

Date	Account Titles and Explanation	PR	Debit	Credit
a.				
b.				
c.				
d.				
e.				

Analysis component:

_____
_____
_____
_____
_____
_____
_____

ACCOUNT	UNADJUSTED TRIAL BALANCE		ADJUSTMENTS		ADJUSTED TRIAL BALANCE	
	Debit	Credit	Debit	Credit	Debit	Credit
Cash	$ 3,500					
Accounts receivable	7,200					
Prepaid advertising	-0-					
Cleaning supplies	-0-					
Equipment	29,000					
Accum. deprec., equipment		$ 3,200				
Unearned window washing fees		-0-				
Unearned office cleaning fees		-0-				
Wllllam Nahanee, capital		9,150				
Window washing fees earned		23,800				
Office cleaning fees earned		71,500				
Advertlsing expense	2,900					
Salaries expense	56,900					
Depreciation expense, equip.	-0-					
Cleaning supplies expense	8,150					
Totals	$107,650	$107,650				

*Problem 3-17B

Part 1 - Entries that initially recognize assets and liabilities:

GENERAL JOURNAL   Page_____

Date	Account Titles and Explanation	PR	Debit	Credit

GENERAL JOURNAL   Page____

Date	Account Titles and Explanation	PR	Debit	Credit

Part 2 – Entries that initially recognize expenses and revenues:

GENERAL JOURNAL   Page____

Date	Account Titles and Explanation	PR	Debit	Credit

Part 2 (concl'd)

GENERAL JOURNAL   Page____

Date		Account Titles and Explanation	PR	Debit	Credit

Analysis component:

_____
_____
_____
_____
_____
_____
_____
_____
_____
_____
_____
_____
_____

GENERAL JOURNAL   Page _____

Date	Account Titles and Explanation	PR	Debit	Credit

GENERAL JOURNAL   Page _____

Date	Account Titles and Explanation	PR	Debit	Credit

GENERAL LEDGER

Cash   ACCOUNT NO. 101

DATE	EXPLANATION	PR	DEBIT	CREDIT	BALANCE
2014 Nov. 30	Balance				70,340

Accounts Receivable   ACCOUNT NO. 106

DATE	EXPLANATION	PR	DEBIT	CREDIT	BALANCE
2014 Nov. 30	Balance				18,900

Computer Supplies   ACCOUNT NO. 126

DATE	EXPLANATION	PR	DEBIT	CREDIT	BALANCE
2014 Nov. 30	Balance				4,560

Prepaid Insurance   ACCOUNT NO. 128

DATE	EXPLANATION	PR	DEBIT	CREDIT	BALANCE
2014 Nov. 30	Balance				4,320

Prepaid Rent   ACCOUNT NO. 131

DATE	EXPLANATION	PR	DEBIT	CREDIT	BALANCE
2014 Nov. 30	Balance				9,000

Part 2   Echo Systems (Cont'd.)

Office Equipment   ACCOUNT NO. 163

DATE	EXPLANATION	PR	DEBIT	CREDIT	BALANCE
2014 Nov. 30	Balance				18,000

Accumulated Depreciation, Office Equipment   ACCOUNT NO. 164

DATE	EXPLANATION	PR	DEBIT	CREDIT	BALANCE
2014 Nov. 30	Balance				-0-

Computer Equipment   ACCOUNT NO. 167

DATE	EXPLANATION	PR	DEBIT	CREDIT	BALANCE
2014 Nov. 30	Balance				36,000

Accumulated Depreciation, Computer Equipment   ACCOUNT NO. 168

DATE	EXPLANATION	PR	DEBIT	CREDIT	BALANCE
2014 Nov. 30	Balance				-0-

Accounts Payable   ACCOUNT NO. 201

DATE	EXPLANATION	PR	DEBIT	CREDIT	BALANCE
2014 Nov. 30	Balance				-0-

Wages Payable   ACCOUNT NO. 210

DATE	EXPLANATION	PR	DEBIT	CREDIT	BALANCE
2014 Nov. 30	Balance				-0-

Unearned Computer Services Revenue   ACCOUNT NO. 236

DATE	EXPLANATION	PR	DEBIT	CREDIT	BALANCE
2014 Nov. 30	Balance				-0-

Mary Graham, Capital   ACCOUNT NO. 301

DATE	EXPLANATION	PR	DEBIT	CREDIT	BALANCE
2014 Nov. 30	Balance				144,000

Chapter 3   Serial Problem   *Name* _____

Part 2   Echo Systems (Cont'd.)

Mary Graham, Withdrawals   ACCOUNT NO. 302

DATE	EXPLANATION	PR	DEBIT	CREDIT	BALANCE
2014 Nov. 30	Balance				10,800

Computer Services Revenue   ACCOUNT NO. 403

DATE	EXPLANATION	PR	DEBIT	CREDIT	BALANCE
2014 Nov. 30	Balance				40,950

Depreciation Expense, Office Equipment   ACCOUNT NO. 612

DATE	EXPLANATION	PR	DEBIT	CREDIT	BALANCE
2014 Nov. 30	Balance				-0-

Depreciation Expense, Computer Equipment   ACCOUNT NO. 613

DATE	EXPLANATION	PR	DEBIT	CREDIT	BALANCE
2014 Nov. 30	Balance				-0-

Wages Expense   ACCOUNT NO. 623

DATE	EXPLANATION	PR	DEBIT	CREDIT	BALANCE
2014 Nov. 30	Balance				4,200

Insurance Expense   ACCOUNT NO. 637

DATE	EXPLANATION	PR	DEBIT	CREDIT	BALANCE
2014 Nov. 30	Balance				-0-

Rent Expense   ACCOUNT NO. 640

DATE	EXPLANATION	PR	DEBIT	CREDIT	BALANCE
2014 Nov. 30	Balance				-0-

Computer Supplies Expense   ACCOUNT NO. 652

DATE	EXPLANATION	PR	DEBIT	CREDIT	BALANCE
2014 Nov. 30	Balance				-0-

Advertising Expense   ACCOUNT NO. 655

DATE	EXPLANATION	PR	DEBIT	CREDIT	BALANCE
2014 Nov. 30	Balance				3,720

Mileage Expense   ACCOUNT NO. 676

DATE	EXPLANATION	PR	DEBIT	CREDIT	BALANCE
2014 Nov. 30	Balance				2,200

Repairs Expense, Computer   ACCOUNT NO. 684

DATE	EXPLANATION	PR	DEBIT	CREDIT	BALANCE
2014 Nov. 30	Balance				1,410

Charitable Donations Expense   ACCOUNT NO. 699

DATE	EXPLANATION	PR	DEBIT	CREDIT	BALANCE
2014 Nov. 30	Balance				1,500

ECHO SYSTEMS
Adjusted Trial Balance
December 31, 2014

	Debit	Credit

ECHO SYSTEMS
Income Statement
For Three Months Ended December 31, 2014

ECHO SYSTEMS
Statement of Changes in Equity
For Three Months Ended December 31, 2014

ECHO SYSTEMS
Balance Sheet
December 31, 2014

Chapter 4   Quick Study 4-1   *Name* _____

1. _____ Equipment
2. _____ Owner, withdrawals
3. _____ Insurance expense
4. _____ Prepaid insurance
5. _____ Accounts receivable
6. _____ Depreciation expense, equipment

Quick Study 4-2

- see next page for QS 4-2 working paper

Quick Study 4-3

_____
_____
_____
_____
_____
_____
_____
_____
_____

Quick Study 4-4

_____
_____
_____
_____
_____
_____
_____

Quick Study 4-5

_____
_____
_____
_____
_____
_____
_____
_____
_____
_____
_____
_____
_____

Account Title	Unadjusted Trial Balance		Adjustments		Adjusted Trial Balance		Income Statement		Balance Sheet & Statement of Changes in Equity	
	Debit	Credit	Debit	Credit	Debit	Credit	Debit	Credit	Debit	Credit
Cash	15									
Accounts receivable	22									
Supplies	25			8						
Ed Wolt, capital		40								
Ed Wolt, withdrawals	12									
Fees earned		48								
Supplies expense			8							
Totals	88	88	8	8						

GENERAL JOURNAL   Page____

Date	Account Titles and Explanation	PR	Debit	Credit

Assets
250

Liabilities
30

Capital
200

Withdrawals
20

Expenses
60

Revenue
100

Income Summary

GENERAL JOURNAL   Page____

Date	Account Titles and Explanation	PR	Debit	Credit

Assets
250

Liabilities
110

Capital
200

Withdrawals
20

Expenses
140

Revenue
100

Income Summary

Post-Closing Trial Balance

	Debit	Credit

Quick Study 4-9

a. _____ Preparing the unadjusted trial balance.
b. _____ Preparing the post-closing trial balance.
c. _____ Journalizing and posting adjusting entries.
d. _____ Journalizing and posting closing entries.
e. _____ Preparing the financial statements.
f. _____ Journalizing transactions.
g. _____ Posting the transaction entries.
h. _____ Completing the work sheet.

Quick Study 4-10

1. _____ Store equipment
2. _____ Wages payable
3. _____ Cash
4. _____ Notes payable (due in three years)
5. _____ Land not currently used in business operations
6. _____ Accounts receivable
7. _____ Trademarks

Chapter 4   Quick Study 4-11   *Name* _____

1. ____ Depreciation expense, trucks
2. ____ Lee Hale, capital
3. ____ Interest receivable
4. ____ Lee Hale, withdrawals
5. ____ Automobiles
6. ____ Notes payable (due in 3 years)
7. ____ Accounts payable
8. ____ Prepaid insurance
9. ____ Land not currently used in business operations
10. ____ Unearned services revenue
11. ____ Accum. deprec., trucks
12. ____ Cash
13. ____ Building
14. ____ Patent
15. ____ Office equipment
16. ____ Land (used in operations)
17. ____ Repairs expense
18. ____ Prepaid property taxes
19. ____ Notes payable (due in 2 months)
20. ____ Notes receivable (due in 2 years)

Quick Study 4-12

Partial Balance Sheet

*Quick Study 4-13

GENERAL JOURNAL   Page____

Date	Account Titles and Explanation	PR	Debit	Credit

_____
_____
_____
_____
_____

Exercise 4-1

1. _____ Roberta Jefferson, withdrawals	9. _____ Cash
2. _____ Interest earned	10. _____ Office supplies
3. _____ Accum. deprec., machinery	11. _____ Roberta Jefferson, capital
4. _____ Service fees revenue	12. _____ Wages payable
5. _____ Accounts receivable	13. _____ Machinery
6. _____ Rent expense	14. _____ Insurance expense
7. _____ Deprec. exp., machinery	15. _____ Interest expense
8. _____ Accounts payable	16. _____ Interest receivable

Exercise 4-2

ACCOUNT	ADJUSTED TRIAL BALANCE Debit	ADJUSTED TRIAL BALANCE Credit	INCOME STATEMENT Debit	INCOME STATEMENT Credit	BALANCE SHEET AND STATEMENT OF CHANGES IN EQUITY Debit	BALANCE SHEET AND STATEMENT OF CHANGES IN EQUITY Credit
Cash	21,000					
Accounts receivable	8,200					
Trucks	48,000					
Accum. deprec., trucks		31,250				
Franchise	6,500					
Accounts payable		13,000				
Salaries payable		14,600				
Unearned fees		2,450				
Bo Webber, capital		37,750				
Bo Webber, withdrls.	7,200					
Plumbing fees earned		31,600				
Deprec. expense, trucks	12,100					
Salaries expense	17,800					
Rent expense	6,000					
Miscellaneous expense	3,850					
Totals	130,650	130,650				

Parts 1, 2, and 3

Musical Sensations

Work Sheet

For Year Ended December 31, 2014

Account Title	Unadjusted Trial Balance		Adjustments		Adjusted Trial Balance		Income Statement		Balance Sheet and Statement of Changes in Equity	
	Debit	Credit	Debit	Credit	Debit	Credit	Debit	Credit	Debit	Credit
Cash	7,500									
Accounts receivable	14,200									
Office supplies	790									
Musical equipment	125,000									
Accum. dep., musical equip.		21,600								
Accounts payable		4,200								
Unearned performance rev.		12,400								
Jim Daley, capital		154,300								
Jim Daley, withdrawals	52,000									
Performance revenue		138,000								
Salaries expense	86,000									
Travelling expense	45,010									
Totals	330,500	330,500								

Part 4

_____
_____   **Jim Daley, Capital**
_____   _____|_____
_____ |
_____ |
_____ |

Exercise 4-4

1(a) _____

2(a)   **GENERAL JOURNAL**   Page____

Date	Account Titles and Explanation	PR	Debit	Credit

3(a)   **Owner's Capital**

_____   _____|_____
_____ |
_____ |
_____ |

1(b) _____

2(b)   **GENERAL JOURNAL**   Page____

Date	Account Titles and Explanation	PR	Debit	Credit

3(b)   **Owner's Capital**

_____   _____|_____
_____ |
_____ |
_____ |

	Debit	Credit
Rent earned		99,000
Salaries expense	35,300	
Insurance expense	4,400	
Dock rental expense	12,000	
Boat supplies expense	6,220	
Depreciation expense, boats	21,500	_____
Totals		
Net income	_____	_____
Totals	======	======

Closing Entries

GENERAL JOURNAL   Page____

Date	Account Titles and Explanation	PR	Debit	Credit

GENERAL JOURNAL   Page____

Date	Account Titles and Explanation	PR	Debit	Credit

Post-Closing Trial Balance

	Debit	Credit

GENERAL JOURNAL   Page____

Date	Account Titles and Explanation	PR	Debit	Credit

Exercise 4-8

GENERAL JOURNAL   Page____

Date	Account Titles and Explanation	PR	Debit	Credit

GENERAL JOURNAL   Page____

Date	Account Titles and Explanation	PR	Debit	Credit

Exercise 4-10

GENERAL JOURNAL   Page____

Date	Account Titles and Explanation	PR	Debit	Credit

Posting to Accounts:

Assets		Liabilities	
Bal. Dec. 31 142,000		51,000 Bal. Dec. 31	

Marcy Jones, Capital		Marcy Jones, Withdrawals	
	71,800 Bal. Dec. 31	Bal. Dec. 31 38,000	

Services Revenue		Salaries Expense	
	103,000 Bal. Dec. 31	Bal. Dec. 31 27,000	

Rent Expense		Insurance Expense	
Bal. Dec. 31 9,100		Bal. Dec. 31 1,500	

Depreciation Expense		Income Summary	
Bal. Dec. 31 8,200			

Exercise 4-11

Post-Closing Trial Balance

	Debit	Credit

Chapter 4   Exercise 4-12   *Name* _____

1. _____

2.   GENERAL JOURNAL   Page____

Date	Account Titles and Explanation	PR	Debit	Credit

3.

Bill Duggan, Capital

Exercise 4-13

a.

Account Title	Adjusted Trial Balance Debit	Credit
Accounts payable		$ 31,000
Accounts receivable	$ 48,000	
Accumulated depreciation, equipment		9,000
Accumulated depreciation, truck		21,000
Cash	14,400	
Depreciation expense	3,800	
Equipment	19,000	
Franchise	21,000	
Gas and oil expense	7,500	
Interest expense	450	
Interest payable		750
Land not currently used in business operations	148,000	
Long-term notes payable		35,000
Notes payable, due February 1, 2015		7,000
Notes receivable	6,000	
Patent	7,000	
Prepaid Rent	14,000	
Rent expense	51,000	
Repair revenue		266,000
Repair supplies	13,100	
Repair supplies expense	29,000	
Truck	26,000	
Unearned repair revenue		12,600
Vic Sopik, capital		74,900
Vic Sopik, withdrawals	49,000	
Totals	$457,250	$457,250

b.   **Vic Sopik, Capital**

Analysis component: _____

_____

_____

_____

Exercise 4-14   **Calculations:**

a.   **Current assets =**

b.   **Property, plant and equipment =**

c.   **Intangible assets =**

d.   **Long-term investments =**

e.   **Total assets =**

f.   **Current liabilities =**

g.   **Long-term liabilities =**

h.   **Total liabilities =**

i.   **Total liabilities and equity =**

Balance Sheet

Balance Sheet

a. _____

_____

_____

_____

b. Journalizing:

GENERAL JOURNAL   Page____

Date	Account Titles and Explanation	PR	Debit	Credit

c. _____

Unadjusted Trial Balance

	Debit	Credit

b, d, g. Posting journal entries in (b), adjustments in (d), and closing entries in (g):

Cash

Bal. Dec. 31/13 **2,000**	

Leda Svenson, Capital

	17,100 Bal. Dec. 31/13

Accounts Receivable

Bal. Dec. 31/13 **5,000**	

Leda Svenson, Withdrawals

Bal. Dec. 31/13 **-0-**	

Tutoring Fees Earned

	-0- Bal. Dec. 31/13

Prepaid Rent

Bal. Dec. 31/13 **3,000**	

Office Equipment

Bal. Dec. 31/13 **20,000**	

Rent Expense

Bal. Dec. 31/13 **-0-**	

Accum. Deprec., Office Equip.

	10,000 Bal. Dec. 31/13

Depreciation Expense

Bal. Dec. 31/13 **-0-**	

Unearned Fees

	2,900 Bal. Dec. 31/13

Advertising Expense

Bal. Dec. 31/13 **-0-**	

Income Summary

d. Journalize adjustments:

GENERAL JOURNAL   Page____

Date	Account Titles and Explanation	PR	Debit	Credit

e. _____

Adjusted Trial Balance

	Debit	Credit

Chapter 4   Exercise 4-17 (cont'd.)   *Name* _____

f. Financial statement preparation:

Income Statement

Statement of Changes in Equity

Balance Sheet

g. Journalize closing entries:

GENERAL JOURNAL

Page____

Date	Account Titles and Explanation	PR	Debit	Credit

h. _____

Post-Closing Trial Balance

	Debit	Credit

GENERAL JOURNAL   Page____

Date	Account Titles and Explanation	PR	Debit	Credit

*Exercise 4-19

1. Adjusting entries:

GENERAL JOURNAL   Page _____

Date	Account Titles and Explanation	PR	Debit	Credit

2. Subsequent entries without reversing:

GENERAL JOURNAL   Page _____

Date	Account Titles and Explanation	PR	Debit	Credit

GENERAL JOURNAL   Page _____

Date	Account Titles and Explanation	PR	Debit	Credit

3. Reversing entries and subsequent entries:

GENERAL JOURNAL   Page _____

Date	Account Titles and Explanation	PR	Debit	Credit

_____
_____
_____
_____
_____
_____
_____
_____
_____
_____
_____
_____
_____
_____
_____
_____
_____

Nanimahco Rentals

Work Sheet

For Year Ended March 31, 2014

Account Title	Unadjusted Trial Balance Debit	Unadjusted Trial Balance Credit	Adjustments Debit	Adjustments Credit	Adjusted Trial Balance Debit	Adjusted Trial Balance Credit	Income Statement Debit	Income Statement Credit	Balance Sheet and Statement of Changes in Equity Debit	Balance Sheet and Statement of Changes in Equity Credit
Cash	7,000									
Rent receivable	31,000									
Office supplies	2,250									
Notes receivable, due 2017	46,000									
Furniture	16,000									
Building	216,000									
Land	41,000									
Patent	9,600									
Accounts payable		13,750								
Long-term note payable		175,000								
Joan Nanimahoo, capital		90,250								
Joan Nanimahoo, withdrawals	92,000									
Rent earned		328,800								
Office salaries expense	52,000									
Interest expense	5,250									
Advertising expense	14,600									
Janitorial expense	41,000									
Utilities expense	34,100									
Totals	607,800	607,800								

Trenton Consulting

Work Sheet

For Year Ended June 30, 2014

Account Title	Unadjusted Trial Balance		Adjustments		Adjusted Trial Balance		Income Statement		Balance Sheet and Statement of Changes in Equity	
	Debit	Credit	Debit	Credit	Debit	Credit	Debit	Credit	Debit	Credit
Cash	680									
Accounts receivable	2,900									
Prepaid rent	3,660									
Equipment	9,600									
Accounts payable		1,730								
Toni Trenton, capital		26,650								
Toni Trenton, withdrawals	6,880									
Consulting fees earned		30,200								
Wages expense	24,920									
Insurance expense	1,620									
Rent expense	8,320									
Totals	58,580	58,580								

Part 4

_____   **Toni Trenton, Capital**
_____   _____
_____
_____

Analysis component:

_____
_____
_____
_____
_____
_____

Part 1

Challenger Construction

Work Sheet

For Year Ended September 30, 2014

Account Title	Unadjusted Trial Balance		Adjustments		Adjusted Trial Balance		Income Statement		Balance Sheet and Statement of Changes in Equity	
	Debit	Credit	Debit	Credit	Debit	Credit	Debit	Credit	Debit	Credit
Cash	22,000									
Supplies	17,200									
Prepaid insurance	9,600									
Land not currently used	50,000									
Equipment	106,000									
Accum. deprec., equipment		40,500								
Copyright	6,000									
Accounts payable		8,100								
Interest payable										
Wages payable										
Long-term notes payable		50,000								
Chris Challenger, capital		71,000								
Chris Challenger, withdrawals	68,000									
Construction fees earned		255,620								
Deprec. Expense, equipment										
Wages expense	96,000									
Interest expense	1,200									
Insurance expense										
Rent expense	26,400									
Supplies expense										
Business taxes expense	10,000									
Repairs expense	5,020									
Utilities expense	7,800									
Totals	425,220	425,220								

Part 2
Adjusting entries:

GENERAL JOURNAL   Page____

Date	Account Titles and Explanation	PR	Debit	Credit
a.				
b.				
c.				
d.				
e.				
f.				

Part 2
Closing entries:

GENERAL JOURNAL

Date	Account Titles and Explanation	PR	Debit	Credit

Part 3

Income Statement

Statement of Changes in Equity

Balance Sheet			

Analysis component:

a. _____

_____

_____

b. _____

_____

_____

Part 1   **GENERAL JOURNAL**   Page____

Date	Account Titles and Explanation	PR	Debit	Credit

Part 2

Post-Closing Trial Balance

Income Statement

Statement of Changes in Equity

Balance Sheet

Analysis component:

_____
_____
_____
_____
_____
_____
_____
_____

Name: _____

GENERAL JOURNAL

Page____

Date	Account Titles and Explanation	PR	Debit	Credit

Income Statement

Statement of Changes in Equity

Balance Sheet

Analysis component:

_____
_____
_____
_____

GENERAL JOURNAL   Page____

Date	Account Titles and Explanation	PR	Debit	Credit

Income Statement

Statement of Changes in Equity

Balance Sheet

Analysis component:

_____
_____
_____
_____
_____
_____
_____

Part 1

	Income Statement		

Part 2

_____

_____

_____

_____

Noel Apex, Capital

Income Statement

Statement of Changes in Equity

Balance Sheet

Analysis component:

_____

_____

_____

_____

_____

Part 1

_____   _____
_____   **Wyett North, Capital**
_____   _____
_____

Part 2

_____

Balance Sheet

_____

Analysis component:

_____
_____
_____
_____
_____
_____

Part 1. Use either the balance column format or T-accounts; both are provided.

GENERAL LEDGER

Cash   ACCOUNT NO. 101

DATE	EXPLANATION	PR	DEBIT	CREDIT	BALANCE

Accounts Receivable   ACCOUNT NO. 106

DATE	EXPLANATION	PR	DEBIT	CREDIT	BALANCE

Office Supplies   ACCOUNT NO. 124

DATE	EXPLANATION	PR	DEBIT	CREDIT	BALANCE

Prepaid Insurance   ACCOUNT NO. 128

DATE	EXPLANATION	PR	DEBIT	CREDIT	BALANCE

Furniture   ACCOUNT NO. 160

DATE	EXPLANATION	PR	DEBIT	CREDIT	BALANCE

Accumulated Depreciation, Furniture   ACCOUNT NO. 161

DATE	EXPLANATION	PR	DEBIT	CREDIT	BALANCE

Computer Equipment   ACCOUNT NO. 167

DATE	EXPLANATION	PR	DEBIT	CREDIT	BALANCE

Accumulated Depreciation, Computer Equipment   ACCOUNT NO. 168

DATE	EXPLANATION	PR	DEBIT	CREDIT	BALANCE

Accounts Payable   ACCOUNT NO. 201

DATE	EXPLANATION	PR	DEBIT	CREDIT	BALANCE

Salaries Payable   ACCOUNT NO. 209

DATE	EXPLANATION	PR	DEBIT	CREDIT	BALANCE

Sam Near, Capital   ACCOUNT NO. 301

DATE	EXPLANATION	PR	DEBIT	CREDIT	BALANCE

Sam Near, Withdrawals   ACCOUNT NO. 302

DATE	EXPLANATION	PR	DEBIT	CREDIT	BALANCE

Commissions Earned   ACCOUNT NO. 405

DATE	EXPLANATION	PR	DEBIT	CREDIT	BALANCE

Depreciation Expense, Furniture   ACCOUNT NO. 610

DATE	EXPLANATION	PR	DEBIT	CREDIT	BALANCE

Depreciation Expense, Computer Equipment   ACCOUNT NO. 612

DATE	EXPLANATION	PR	DEBIT	CREDIT	BALANCE

Salaries Expense   ACCOUNT NO. 622

DATE	EXPLANATION	PR	DEBIT	CREDIT	BALANCE

Insurance Expense   ACCOUNT NO. 637

DATE	EXPLANATION	PR	DEBIT	CREDIT	BALANCE

Rent Expense   ACCOUNT NO. 640

DATE	EXPLANATION	PR	DEBIT	CREDIT	BALANCE

Office Supplies Expense   ACCOUNT NO. 650

DATE	EXPLANATION	PR	DEBIT	CREDIT	BALANCE

Repairs Expense   ACCOUNT NO. 684

DATE	EXPLANATION	PR	DEBIT	CREDIT	BALANCE

Telephone Expense   ACCOUNT NO. 688

DATE	EXPLANATION	PR	DEBIT	CREDIT	BALANCE

	Income Summary				ACCOUNT NO. 901
DATE	EXPLANATION	PR	DEBIT	CREDIT	BALANCE

Part 1. Use either T-accounts or the balance column format; both are provided.

Cash   101

Accounts Receivable   106

Office Supplies   124

Prepaid Insurance   128

Furniture   160

Accum. Deprec, Furniture   161

Computer Equipment   167

Accum. Deprec, Computer Equip   168

Accounts Payable   201

Salaries Payable   209

Sam Near, Capital   301

Sam Near, Withdrawals   302

Commissions Earned   405

Part 1. Use either T-accounts or the balance column format; both are provided.

Deprec. Exp, Furniture 610	Office Supplies Expense 650

Deprec. Exp, Computer Equip. 612	Repairs Expense 684

Salaries Expense 622	Telephone Expense 688

Insurance Expense 637	Income Summary 901

Rent Expense 640	

Part 2. Transactions for June:

GENERAL JOURNAL

Page____

Date	Account Titles and Explanation	PR	Debit	Credit

Part 2. Transactions for June (cont'd.)

GENERAL JOURNAL   Page____

Date	Account Titles and Explanation	PR	Debit	Credit

Part 3. Adjusting entries:

GENERAL JOURNAL   Page____

Date	Account Titles and Explanation	PR	Debit	Credit

Part 4

Income Statement

Statement of Changes in Equity

Balance Sheet

Part 5. Closing entries:

GENERAL JOURNAL   Page____

Date	Account Titles and Explanation	PR	Debit	Credit

Part 6

Post-Closing Trial Balance

	Debit	Credit

Part 1

GENERAL JOURNAL   Page____

Date	Account Titles and Explanation	PR	Debit	Credit
a.				
b.				
c.				
d.				
e.				
f.				

Part 2

GENERAL JOURNAL   Page____

Date	Account Titles and Explanation	PR	Debit	Credit

Part 3

GENERAL JOURNAL   Page____

Date	Account Titles and Explanation	PR	Debit	Credit

Parts 1, 2, and 3

Daimler Tours

Work Sheet

For Year Ended July 31, 2014

Account Title	Unadjusted Trial Balance		Adjustments		Adjusted Trial Balance		Income Statement		Balance Sheet and Statement of Changes in Equity	
	Debit	Credit	Debit	Credit	Debit	Credit	Debit	Credit	Debit	Credit
Cash	9,100									
Accounts receivable	18,700									
Notes receivable	16,000									
Prepaid insurance	5,100									
Furniture	6,750									
Accounts payable		6,925								
Unearned tour revenue		12,430								
Jan Rider, capital		60,975								
Jan Rider, withdrawals	-0-									
Tour revenue		16,700								
Wages expense	41,380									
Totals	97,030	97,030								

Parts 1, 2, and 3

Tucker Photographers

Work Sheet

For Year Ended December 31, 2014

Account Title	Unadjusted Trial Balance		Adjustments		Adjusted Trial Balance		Income Statement		Balance Sheet and Statement of Changes in Equity	
	Debit	Credit	Debit	Credit	Debit	Credit	Debit	Credit	Debit	Credit
Cash	9,100									
Accounts receivable	13,000									
Prepaid equipment rental	3,860									
Automobile	49,000									
Accum. deprec., automobile		-0-								
Accounts payable		1,920								
Unearned fees		5,740								
Jim Tucker, capital		65,700								
Jim Tucker, withdrawals	2,600									
Fees earned		8,400								
Deprec. Expense, automobile	-0-									
Equipment rental expense	4,200									
Totals	94,860	94,860								

Part 4

                                            Jim Tucker, Capital

_____

_____

_____

_____

Analysis component:

_____

_____

_____

_____

_____

_____

_____

Part 1

Webster Demolition Company

Work Sheet

For Year Ended June 30, 2014

Account Title	Unadjusted Trial Balance		Adjustments		Adjusted Trial Balance		Income Statement		Balance Sheet and Statement of Changes in Equity	
	Debit	Credit	Debit	Credit	Debit	Credit	Debit	Credit	Debit	Credit
Cash	4,500									
Supplies	8,200									
Prepaid insurance	7,300									
Equipment	72,000									
Accum. deprec., equipment		5,000								
Accounts payable		9,100								
Interest payable										
Wages payable										
Long-term notes payable		45,000								
Rusty Webster, capital		21,400								
Rusty Webster, withdrawals	2,100									
Demolition fees earned		83,300								
Deprec. expense, equipment										
Wages expense	27,400									
Interest expense	1,100									
Insurance expense										
Rent expense	24,400									
Supplies expense										
Business tax expense	4,200									
Repairs expense	4,200									
Utilities expense	8,400									
Totals	163,800	163,800								

Part 2
Adjusting entries:

GENERAL JOURNAL   Page____

Date	Account Titles and Explanation	PR	Debit	Credit
a.				
b.				
c.				
d.				
e.				
f.				

Part 2
Closing entries:

GENERAL JOURNAL   Page____

Date	Account Titles and Explanation	PR	Debit	Credit

Part 3

Income Statement

Statement of Changes in Equity

Balance Sheet			

Analysis component:

a. _____

_____

_____

b. _____

_____

_____

Part 1　　　　　　　　　　GENERAL JOURNAL　　　　　　Page____

Date	Account Titles and Explanation	PR	Debit	Credit

Part 2

Post-Closing Trial Balance

	Debit	Credit

Income Statement

Statement of Changes in Equity

Balance Sheet

Analysis component:

_____

_____

_____

_____

GENERAL JOURNAL   Page____

Date	Account Titles and Explanation	PR	Debit	Credit

Income Statement

Statement of Changes in Equity

Balance Sheet

Analysis component:

GENERAL JOURNAL   Page____

Date	Account Titles and Explanation	PR	Debit	Credit

Chapter 4   Problem 4-9B   *Name* _____

Income Statement

Statement of Changes in Equity

Balance Sheet

Analysis component:

_____

_____

_____

_____

_____

Part 1

Income Statement		

Part 2

	Grant Greenway, Capital
_____	
_____	
_____	
_____	

Income Statement

Statement of Changes in Equity

Balance Sheet

Analysis component:

_____
_____
_____
_____
_____
_____

Part 1

_____   **Jan Delta, Capital**
_____   _____|_____
_____ |
_____ |
                                                           |

Part 2

_____
_____

Balance Sheet

Part 1. Use either the balance column format or T-accounts; both are provided.

GENERAL LEDGER

Cash   ACCOUNT NO. 101

DATE	EXPLANATION	PR	DEBIT	CREDIT	BALANCE

Accounts Receivable   ACCOUNT NO. 106

DATE	EXPLANATION	PR	DEBIT	CREDIT	BALANCE

Office Supplies   ACCOUNT NO. 124

DATE	EXPLANATION	PR	DEBIT	CREDIT	BALANCE

Prepaid Insurance   ACCOUNT NO. 128

DATE	EXPLANATION	PR	DEBIT	CREDIT	BALANCE

Land   ACCOUNT NO. 170

DATE	EXPLANATION	PR	DEBIT	CREDIT	BALANCE

Buildings   ACCOUNT NO. 173

DATE	EXPLANATION	PR	DEBIT	CREDIT	BALANCE

Accumulated Depreciation, Buildings   ACCOUNT NO. 174

DATE	EXPLANATION	PR	DEBIT	CREDIT	BALANCE

Accounts Payable   ACCOUNT NO. 201

DATE	EXPLANATION	PR	DEBIT	CREDIT	BALANCE

Salaries Payable   ACCOUNT NO. 209

DATE	EXPLANATION	PR	DEBIT	CREDIT	BALANCE

Amy Young, Capital   ACCOUNT NO. 301

DATE	EXPLANATION	PR	DEBIT	CREDIT	BALANCE

Amy Young, Withdrawals   ACCOUNT NO. 302

DATE	EXPLANATION	PR	DEBIT	CREDIT	BALANCE

Storage Fees Earned   ACCOUNT NO. 401

DATE	EXPLANATION	PR	DEBIT	CREDIT	BALANCE

Depreciation Expense, Buildings   ACCOUNT NO. 606

DATE	EXPLANATION	PR	DEBIT	CREDIT	BALANCE

Salaries Expense   ACCOUNT NO. 622

DATE	EXPLANATION	PR	DEBIT	CREDIT	BALANCE

Insurance Expense   ACCOUNT NO. 637

DATE	EXPLANATION	PR	DEBIT	CREDIT	BALANCE

Equipment Rental Expense   ACCOUNT NO. 640

DATE	EXPLANATION	PR	DEBIT	CREDIT	BALANCE

Office Supplies Expense   ACCOUNT NO. 650

DATE	EXPLANATION	PR	DEBIT	CREDIT	BALANCE

Repairs Expense   ACCOUNT NO. 684

DATE	EXPLANATION	PR	DEBIT	CREDIT	BALANCE

Telephone Expense   ACCOUNT NO. 688

DATE	EXPLANATION	PR	DEBIT	CREDIT	BALANCE

Income Summary   ACCOUNT NO. 901

DATE	EXPLANATION	PR	DEBIT	CREDIT	BALANCE

Cash	101

Accounts Payable	201

Salaries Payable	209

Amy Young, Capital	301

Accounts Receivable	106

Amy Young, Withdrawals	302

Storage Fees Earned	405

Office Supplies	124

Prepaid Insurance	128

Deprec. Exp., Buildings	606

Salaries Expense	622

Land	170

Insurance Expense	637

Buildings	173

Accum. Deprec., Buildings	174

Equipment Rental Expense	640

Office Supplies Expense	650

Telephone Expense	688

Repairs Expense	684

Income Summary	901

Part 2. Transactions for July:

GENERAL JOURNAL   Page____

Date	Account Titles and Explanation	PR	Debit	Credit

Part 2. Transactions for July (cont'd.)

GENERAL JOURNAL   Page____

Date	Account Titles and Explanation	PR	Debit	Credit

Part 3. Adjusting entries:

GENERAL JOURNAL   Page____

Date	Account Titles and Explanation	PR	Debit	Credit

Part 4

Income Statement

Statement of Changes in Equity

Balance Sheet

Chapter 4   Problem 4-13B (concl'd.)   *Name* _____

Part 5. Closing entries:

GENERAL JOURNAL   Page____

Date	Account Titles and Explanation	PR	Debit	Credit

Part 6

Post-Closing Trial Balance

	Debit	Credit

Part 1

GENERAL JOURNAL   Page____

Date	Account Titles and Explanation	PR	Debit	Credit

Part 2   GENERAL JOURNAL   Page____

Date	Account Titles and Explanation	PR	Debit	Credit

Part 3

GENERAL JOURNAL   Page____

Date	Account Titles and Explanation	PR	Debit	Credit

GENERAL JOURNAL

Date	Account Titles and Explanation	PR	Debit	Credit

GENERAL JOURNAL   Page____

Date	Account Titles and Explanation	PR	Debit	Credit

GENERAL LEDGER

Cash   ACCOUNT NO. 101

DATE	EXPLANATION	PR	DEBIT	CREDIT	BALANCE
2014 Dec. 31	Balance				89,090

Accounts Receivable   ACCOUNT NO. 106

DATE	EXPLANATION	PR	DEBIT	CREDIT	BALANCE
2014 Dec. 31	Balance				5,700

Computer Supplies   ACCOUNT NO. 126

DATE	EXPLANATION	PR	DEBIT	CREDIT	BALANCE
2014 Dec. 31	Balance				1,440

Prepaid Insurance   ACCOUNT NO. 128

DATE	EXPLANATION	PR	DEBIT	CREDIT	BALANCE
2014 Dec. 31	Balance				3,240

Prepaid Rent   ACCOUNT NO. 131

DATE	EXPLANATION	PR	DEBIT	CREDIT	BALANCE
2014 Dec. 31	Balance				2,250

Office Equipment   ACCOUNT NO. 163

DATE	EXPLANATION	PR	DEBIT	CREDIT	BALANCE
2014 Dec. 31	Balance				18,000

Accumulated Depreciation, Office Equipment   ACCOUNT NO. 164

DATE	EXPLANATION	PR	DEBIT	CREDIT	BALANCE
2014 Dec. 31	Balance				1,500

Computer Equipment   ACCOUNT NO. 167

DATE	EXPLANATION	PR	DEBIT	CREDIT	BALANCE
2014 Dec. 31	Balance				36,000

Accumulated Depreciation, Computer Equipment   ACCOUNT NO. 168

DATE	EXPLANATION	PR	DEBIT	CREDIT	BALANCE
2014 Dec. 31	Balance				2,250

Accounts Payable   ACCOUNT NO. 201

DATE	EXPLANATION	PR	DEBIT	CREDIT	BALANCE
2014 Dec. 31	Balance				2,310

Wages Payable   ACCOUNT NO. 210

DATE	EXPLANATION	PR	DEBIT	CREDIT	BALANCE
2014 Dec. 31	Balance				800

Unearned Computer Services Revenue   ACCOUNT NO. 236

DATE	EXPLANATION	PR	DEBIT	CREDIT	BALANCE
2014 Dec. 31	Balance				3,000

Mary Graham, Capital   ACCOUNT NO. 301

DATE	EXPLANATION	PR	DEBIT	CREDIT	BALANCE
2014 Dec. 31	Balance				144,000

Mary Graham, Withdrawals   ACCOUNT NO. 302

DATE	EXPLANATION	PR	DEBIT	CREDIT	BALANCE
2014 Dec. 31	Balance				14,400

Computer Services Revenue   ACCOUNT NO. 403

DATE	EXPLANATION	PR	DEBIT	CREDIT	BALANCE
2014 Dec. 31	Balance				52,200

Depreciation Expense, Office Equipment   ACCOUNT NO. 612

DATE	EXPLANATION	PR	DEBIT	CREDIT	BALANCE
2014 Dec. 31	Balance				1,500

Depreciation Expense, Computer Equipment   ACCOUNT NO. 613

DATE	EXPLANATION	PR	DEBIT	CREDIT	BALANCE
2014 Dec. 31	Balance				2,250

Wages Expense   ACCOUNT NO. 623

DATE	EXPLANATION	PR	DEBIT	CREDIT	BALANCE
2014 Dec. 31	Balance				6,200

Insurance Expense   ACCOUNT NO. 637

DATE	EXPLANATION	PR	DEBIT	CREDIT	BALANCE
2014 Dec. 31	Balance				1,080

Rent Expense   ACCOUNT NO. 640

DATE	EXPLANATION	PR	DEBIT	CREDIT	BALANCE
2014 Dec. 31	Balance				6,750

Computer Supplies Expense   ACCOUNT NO. 652

DATE	EXPLANATION	PR	DEBIT	CREDIT	BALANCE
2014 Dec. 31	Balance				5,430

Advertising Expense   ACCOUNT NO. 655

DATE	EXPLANATION	PR	DEBIT	CREDIT	BALANCE
2014 Dec. 31	Balance				5,820

Mileage Expense   ACCOUNT NO. 676

DATE	EXPLANATION	PR	DEBIT	CREDIT	BALANCE
2014 Dec. 31	Balance				2,800

Repairs Expense, Computer   ACCOUNT NO. 684

DATE	EXPLANATION	PR	DEBIT	CREDIT	BALANCE
2014 Dec. 31	Balance				2,610

Charitable Donations Expense   ACCOUNT NO. 699

DATE	EXPLANATION	PR	DEBIT	CREDIT	BALANCE
2014 Dec. 31	Balance				1,500

Income Summary   ACCOUNT NO. 901

DATE	EXPLANATION	PR	DEBIT	CREDIT	BALANCE
2014 Dec. 31	Balance				

Part 2

ECHO SYSTEMS
Post-Closing Trial Balance
December 31, 2014

	Debit	Credit

	a.	b.	c.	d.	e.
Net sales					
Cost of goods sold					
Gross profit from sales					
Operating expenses					
Net income (loss)					

Quick Study 5-2

a. _____

b. _____

c. _____

d. _____

e. _____

Quick Study 5-3

a. _____

_____

b. _____

_____

Quick Study 5-4

a. _____

_____

b. _____

_____

Quick Study 5-5

GENERAL JOURNAL   Page____

Date	Account Titles and Explanation	PR	Debit	Credit

GENERAL JOURNAL   Page____

Date	Account Titles and Explanation	PR	Debit	Credit

Quick Study 5-6

GENERAL JOURNAL   Page____

Date	Account Titles and Explanation	PR	Debit	Credit

Quick Study 5-7

GENERAL JOURNAL   Page____

Date	Account Titles and Explanation	PR	Debit	Credit

GENERAL JOURNAL   Page____

Date		Account Titles and Explanation	PR	Debit	Credit

Quick Study 5-8

GENERAL JOURNAL   Page____

Date		Account Titles and Explanation	PR	Debit	Credit

GENERAL JOURNAL   Page____

Date		Account Titles and Explanation	PR	Debit	Credit

Quick Study 5-10

GENERAL JOURNAL   Page____

Date		Account Titles and Explanation	PR	Debit	Credit

GENERAL JOURNAL   Page____

Date		Account Titles and Explanation	PR	Debit	Credit

Quick Study 5-11

	(a)	(b)	(c)	(d)

Calculations:

_____

_____

_____

_____

_____

_____

_____

_____

Quick Study 5-12

GENERAL JOURNAL   Page____

Date		Account Titles and Explanation	PR	Debit	Credit

Calculations:

_____

_____

_____

a. Classified Multi-Step

Income Statement

b. Single-Step

Income Statement

_____
_____
_____
_____
_____
_____
_____
_____

Quick Study 5-15

GENERAL JOURNAL   Page_____

Date	Account Titles and Explanation	PR	Debit	Credit

Name _____

a. QS5-5 - Periodic GENERAL JOURNAL Page____

Date	Account Titles and Explanation	PR	Debit	Credit

b. QS5-6 - Periodic GENERAL JOURNAL Page____

Date	Account Titles and Explanation	PR	Debit	Credit

c. QS5-7 - Periodic   GENERAL JOURNAL   Page____

Date	Account Titles and Explanation	PR	Debit	Credit

*Quick Study 5-17

a. QS5-8 - Periodic   GENERAL JOURNAL   Page____

Date	Account Titles and Explanation	PR	Debit	Credit

b. QS5-9 - Periodic   GENERAL JOURNAL   Page____

Date		Account Titles and Explanation	PR	Debit	Credit

c. QS5-10 - Periodic   GENERAL JOURNAL   Page____

Date		Account Titles and Explanation	PR	Debit	Credit

*Quick Study 5-19

GENERAL JOURNAL   Page____

Date	Account Titles and Explanation	PR	Debit	Credit

	(a)	(b)	(c)	(d)

Calculations:

_____

_____

_____

_____

_____

*Quick Study 5-21

GENERAL JOURNAL   Page____

Date	Account Titles and Explanation	PR	Debit	Credit

*Quick Study 5-22

GENERAL JOURNAL   Page____

Date	Account Titles and Explanation	PR	Debit	Credit

GENERAL JOURNAL   Page____

Date	Account Titles and Explanation	PR	Debit	Credit

*Quick Study 5-24

GENERAL JOURNAL   Page____

Date	Account Titles and Explanation	PR	Debit	Credit

Exercise 5-1

	a.	b.	c.	d.	e.
Sales	240,000	140,000	75,000		
Cost of goods sold			42,000	268,000	46,000
Gross profit from sales	114,000				39,000
Operating expenses	95,000	82,000		146,000	
Net income (loss)		(28,000)	(8,000)	48,000	(14,000)

GENERAL JOURNAL   Page_____

Date	Account Titles and Explanation	PR	Debit	Credit

Name _____

GENERAL JOURNAL   Page____

Date	Account Titles and Explanation	PR	Debit	Credit

GENERAL JOURNAL

Page____

Date	Account Titles and Explanation	PR	Debit	Credit

GENERAL JOURNAL   Page____

Date		Account Titles and Explanation	PR	Debit	Credit

GENERAL JOURNAL   Page____

Date	Account Titles and Explanation	PR	Debit	Credit

GENERAL JOURNAL

Page____

Date	Account Titles and Explanation	PR	Debit	Credit
a.	**Purchaser entries (Sundown):**			
b.	**Seller entries (Raintree):**			

Analysis component:

_____
_____
_____
_____
_____
_____
_____
_____
_____
_____

a.   **Entries journalized by Wilson Purchasing:**

GENERAL JOURNAL   Page____

Date	Account Titles and Explanation	PR	Debit	Credit

b.   **Entries journalized by Hostel Sales:**

GENERAL JOURNAL   Page____

Date	Account Titles and Explanation	PR	Debit	Credit

GENERAL JOURNAL

Date	Account Titles and Explanation	PR	Debit	Credit

Analysis component:

_____
_____
_____
_____
_____
_____
_____
_____
_____
_____
_____
_____
_____
_____
_____

Exercise 5-8

1. _____	6. _____
2. _____	7. _____
3. _____	8. _____
4. _____	9. _____
5. _____	10. _____

Merchandise Inventory	Cost of Goods Sold

Analysis component:

_____
_____
_____
_____
_____
_____
_____
_____
_____
_____
_____

Exercise 5-10

a. _____
b. _____
c. _____
d. _____

Analysis component:

_____
_____
_____
_____
_____
_____
_____
_____

	Company A		Company B	
	2014	2013	2014	2013
Sales	$ 256,000	$ 180,000		$ 45,000
Sales discounts	2,560		$ 1,100	500
Sales returns and allowances	_____	16,000	5,500	_____
Net sales		163,000		42,000
Cost of goods sold	153,600	_____	57,000	
Gross profit from sales	51,000	_____	48,400	20,000
Selling expenses	17,920	19,000	25,000	
Administrative expenses	25,600		29,700	9,000
Total operating expenses		46,000		
Net income (loss)		$ 14,400		$ 2,000
Gross profit ratio				

Calculations:

_____
_____
_____
_____
_____
_____

Analysis component:

_____
_____
_____
_____
_____
_____

Exercise 5-12

	(a)	(b)	(c)
Purchases			
Purchases discounts			
Purchase returns and allowances			
Transportation-in			
Cost of goods purchased			
Beginning inventory			
Cost of goods purchased			
Ending inventory			
Cost of goods sold			

	Company A		Company B	
	2014	2013	2014	2013
Sales	110,000	185,000	90,000	
Cost of goods sold:				
Merch. inventory (beginning)	8,700	27,300	8,875	8,000
Net cost of merchandise purchases	62,000			26,100
Merch. Inventory (ending)		(20,000)	(8,920)	(9,875)
Cost of goods sold	64,300	106,000		
Gross profit from sales			39,545	19,775
Operating expenses	26,000	54,000	27,000	
Net income (loss)	1,700	18,000		6,275
Gross profit ratio				

Analysis component:

_____

_____

_____

Exercise 5-14

	(a)	(b)	(c)
Invoice cost of merch. purchases	44,400	21,000	16,250
Purchase discounts	2,000		325
Purchase returns and allowances	1,500	750	550
Cost of transportation-in		1,750	2,000
Merchandise inventory (beginning)	4,500		3,500
Net cost of merchandise purchases	44,700	19,750	
Merchandise inventory (ending)	2,200	3,750	
Cost of goods sold		20,800	17,065

Exercise 5-15

a.

Income Statement

b.   **GENERAL JOURNAL**   Page____

Date	Account Titles and Explanation	PR	Debit	Credit

c: _____   **Peter Delta, Capital**

_____

_____

_____

Analysis component:

_____

_____

_____

_____

_____

_____

_____

Part a

Perdu Sales

Work Sheet

For Year Ended December 31, 2014

Account Title	Unadjusted Trial Balance		Adjustments		Adjusted Trial Balance		Income Statement		Balance Sheet and Statement of Changes in Equity	
	Debit	Credit	Debit	Credit	Debit	Credit	Debit	Credit	Debit	Credit
Cash	8,000									
Merchandise inventory	9,800									
Prepaid selling expenses	8,000									
Store equipment	40,000									
Accum. deprec., store equip.		9,800								
Accounts payable		14,840								
Salaries payable		0								
Eldon Perdu, capital		25,360								
Eldon Perdu, withdrawals	3,600									
Sales		858,000								
Sales returns and allowances	33,000									
Sales discounts	8,000									
Cost of goods sold	431,000									
Sales salaries expense	94,000									
Utilities expense, store	12,600									
Deprec. expense, store equip.										
Other selling expenses	70,000									
Other administrative expenses	190,000									
Totals	908,000	908,000								

Part b

Income Statement

Part c   **GENERAL JOURNAL**   Page____

Date	Account Titles and Explanation	PR	Debit	Credit

GENERAL JOURNAL

Page____

Date	Account Titles and Explanation	PR	Debit	Credit

Analysis component:

_____

_____

_____

_____

_____

_____

Exercise 5-17

a. _____

b. _____

Income Statement

GENERAL JOURNAL

Date	Account Titles and Explanation	PR	Debit	Credit

GENERAL JOURNAL   Page____

Date	Account Titles and Explanation	PR	Debit	Credit

GENERAL JOURNAL

Date	Account Titles and Explanation	PR	Debit	Credit

GENERAL JOURNAL

Date	Account Titles and Explanation	PR	Debit	Credit

GENERAL JOURNAL   Page____

Date	Account Titles and Explanation	PR	Debit	Credit

*Exercise 5-22

GENERAL JOURNAL   Page____

Date	Account Titles and Explanation	PR	Debit	Credit

GENERAL JOURNAL   Page____

Date	Account Titles and Explanation	PR	Debit	Credit

*Exercise 5-23

GENERAL JOURNAL   Page____

Date	Account Titles and Explanation	PR	Debit	Credit
a.	Purchaser entries (Sundown):			
b.	Seller entries (Raintree):			

GENERAL JOURNAL   Page____

Date	Account Titles and Explanation	PR	Debit	Credit

a.

b.

c.

d. _____

_____

Analysis component:

_____

_____

_____

_____

_____

_____

Dewer's Stop'n Shop

Work Sheet

For Year Ended December 31, 2014

Account Title	Unadjusted Trial Balance		Adjustments		Income Statement		Balance Sheet and Statement of Changes in Equity	
	Debit	Credit	Debit	Credit	Debit	Credit	Debit	Credit
Cash	1,400							
Accounts receivable	3,600							
Merchandise inventory	2,700							
Store supplies	1,350							
Accounts payable		280						
Salaries payable								
Mi Dewer, capital		7,220						
Mi Dewer, withdrawals	1,750							
Sales		12,000						
Sales returns and allowances	290							
Purchases	6,400							
Purchase discounts		250						
Transportation-in	160							
Salaries expense	1,600							
Rent expense	500							
Store supplies expense								
Totals	19,750	19,750						

a.

_____
_____
_____
_____
_____
_____

b.

_____
_____
_____
_____
_____
_____

c.

_____
_____
_____
_____
_____
_____

d.

_____

Income Statement

a. _____

b. _____

c. _____

Income Statement

d.   GENERAL JOURNAL   Page____

Date	Account Titles and Explanation	PR	Debit	Credit

e.

_____

_____   **John Yu, Capital**

_____

_____

GENERAL JOURNAL   Page____

Date	Account Titles and Explanation	PR	Debit	Credit

*Exercise 5-30

GENERAL JOURNAL   Page____

Date	Account Titles and Explanation	PR	Debit	Credit

Part 1   GENERAL JOURNAL   Page____

Date	Account Titles and Explanation	PR	Debit	Credit

GENERAL JOURNAL   Page____

Date	Account Titles and Explanation	PR	Debit	Credit

Part 2

_____
_____
_____
_____

Problem 5-2A

GENERAL JOURNAL   Page____

Date	Account Titles and Explanation	PR	Debit	Credit

GENERAL JOURNAL

Page____

Date	Account Titles and Explanation	PR	Debit	Credit

GENERAL JOURNAL   Page____

Date	Account Titles and Explanation	PR	Debit	Credit

Analysis component:

_____
_____
_____
_____
_____
_____
_____
_____
_____
_____
_____

GENERAL JOURNAL   Page____

Date	Account Titles and Explanation	PR	Debit	Credit

GENERAL JOURNAL   Page____

Date	Account Titles and Explanation	PR	Debit	Credit

Part 1

Jumbo's
Work Sheet
For Year Ended December 31, 2014

Account Title	Unadjusted Trial Balance Debit	Unadjusted Trial Balance Credit	Adjustments Debit	Adjustments Credit	Adjusted Trial Balance Debit	Adjusted Trial Balance Credit	Income Statement Debit	Income Statement Credit	Balance Sheet and Statement of Changes in Equity Debit	Balance Sheet and Statement of Changes in Equity Credit
Cash	8,100									
Accounts receivable	22,665									
Merchandise inventory	34,600									
Store supplies	2,415									
Office supplies	775									
Prepaid insurance	3,255									
Equipment	74,490									
Accum. depreciation, equip.		13,655								
Accounts payable		8,000								
Salaries payable										
Sally Fowler, capital		168,965								
Sally Fowler, withdrawals	62,000									
Interest revenue		310								
Sales		529,000								
Sales returns and allowances	5,070									
Cost of goods sold	381,160									
Salaries expenses	96,300									
Rent expense	29,100									
Supplies expense										
Depreciation exp., equipment										
Insurance expense										
Totals	719,930	719,930								

Part 2- Multiple-step

Income Statement

Analysis component:

_____
_____
_____
_____
_____
_____

Part 1 - Classified, multiple-step

Income Statement

Part 2 - Single-step

Income Statement

GENERAL JOURNAL   Page_____

Date	Account Titles and Explanation	PR	Debit	Credit

Part 1 – Classified, multiple-step

Income Statement

Part 2 – Single-step

Income Statement		

Analysis component:

_____
_____
_____
_____
_____
_____
_____
_____

GENERAL JOURNAL

Date		Account Titles and Explanation	PR	Debit	Credit

Part 1 – Classified, multiple-step

Income Statement

Part 2 – Multiple-step

Income Statement

Part 3 – Single-step

Income Statement		

Analysis component:

_____

_____

_____

_____

_____

_____

_____

GENERAL JOURNAL

Page____

Date	Account Titles and Explanation	PR	Debit	Credit

GENERAL JOURNAL

Date	Account Titles and Explanation	PR	Debit	Credit

GENERAL JOURNAL

Date	Account Titles and Explanation	PR	Debit	Credit

1. _____

_____

_____

_____

_____

_____

_____

2. _____

_____

_____

_____

_____

_____

_____

3. _____

_____

_____

_____

_____

_____

_____

_____

_____

_____

_____

4. Multi-step

Income Statement

5. Single-step

Income Statement

GENERAL JOURNAL   Page____

Date	Account Titles and Explanation	PR	Debit	Credit

Part 1

Woodstock Store
Work Sheet
For Year Ended December 31, 2014

Account Title	Unadjusted Trial Balance		Adjustments		Income Statement		Balance Sheet and Statement of Changes in Equity	
	Debit	Credit	Debit	Credit	Debit	Credit	Debit	Credit
Cash	3,500							
Merchandise inventory	31,400							
Store supplies	1,715							
Office supplies	645							
Prepaid insurance	3,960							
Store equipment	57,615							
Accum. deprec., store equip.		6,750						
Office equipment	13,100							
Accum. deprec., office equip.		6,550						
Accounts payable		4,000						
Zen Woodstock, capital		52,000						
Zen Woodstock, withdrawals	31,500							
Rental revenue		14,600						
Sales		501,520						
Sales returns and allowances	2,915							
Sales discounts	5,190							
Purchases	331,315							
Purchase returns and allowances		2,140						
Purchase discounts		4,725						
Transportation-in	3,690							
Sales salaries expenses	34,710							
Rent expense, selling space	24,000							
Advertising expense	6,400							
Store supplies expense								
Deprec. exp., store equipment								
Office salaries expense	27,630							
Rent expense, office space	13,000							
Office supplies expense								
Insurance expense								
Deprec. exp., office equipment								
Totals	592,285	592,?						

Part 2   GENERAL JOURNAL   Page____

Date	Account Titles and Explanation	PR	Debit	Credit

GENERAL LEDGER

Merchandise Inventory   ACCOUNT NO. 110

DATE	EXPLANATION	PR	DEBIT	CREDIT	BALANCE

Income Statement

Name _____

GENERAL JOURNAL   Page___

Date	Account Titles and Explanation	PR	Debit	Credit

GENERAL JOURNAL   Page____

Date	Account Titles and Explanation	PR	Debit	Credit

GENERAL JOURNAL   Page____

Date	Account Titles and Explanation	PR	Debit	Credit

Part 1   **GENERAL JOURNAL**   Page____

Date	Account Titles and Explanation	PR	Debit	Credit

GENERAL JOURNAL   Page____

Date	Account Titles and Explanation	PR	Debit	Credit

Part 2

_____

_____

_____

Problem 5-2B

GENERAL JOURNAL   Page____

Date	Account Titles and Explanation	PR	Debit	Credit

GENERAL JOURNAL

Page____

Date	Account Titles and Explanation	PR	Debit	Credit

GENERAL JOURNAL

Page____

Date	Account Titles and Explanation	PR	Debit	Credit

Analysis component:

_____
_____
_____
_____
_____
_____
_____
_____
_____
_____
_____
_____
_____
_____
_____

GENERAL JOURNAL

Page____

Date	Account Titles and Explanation	PR	Debit	Credit

GENERAL JOURNAL

Page____

Date	Account Titles and Explanation	PR	Debit	Credit

Analysis component:

_____
_____
_____
_____
_____
_____

Part 1

Journey's End Company
Work Sheet
For Year Ended October 31, 2014

Account Title	Unadjusted Trial Balance		Adjustments		Adjusted Trial Balance		Income Statement		Balance Sheet and Statement of Changes in Equity	
	Debit	Credit	Debit	Credit	Debit	Credit	Debit	Credit	Debit	Credit
Cash	12,800									
Merchandise inventory	41,500									
Store supplies	16,700									
Prepaid insurance	5,700									
Store equipment	167,600									
Accum. deprec., store equip.		60,000								
Accounts payable		34,700								
Dallas End, capital		172,100								
Dallas End, withdrawals	12,000									
Sales		391,000								
Sales discounts	3,500									
Sales returns and allowances	8,000									
Cost of goods sold	149,600									
Deprec. expense, store equip.										
Salaries expense	144,000									
Interest expense	800									
Insurance expense										
Rent expense	56,000									
Store supplies expense										
Advertising expense	39,600									
Totals	657,800	657,800								

Part 2

Income Statement

Analysis component:

_____
_____
_____
_____
_____
_____

1. Classified, multiple-step

Income Statement

2. Single-step

Income Statement

GENERAL JOURNAL   Page____

Date	Account Titles and Explanation	PR	Debit	Credit

Part 1 – Classified, multiple-step

Income Statement

Part 2 – Single-step

Income Statement

Analysis component:

_____

_____

_____

_____

GENERAL JOURNAL

Date	Account Titles and Explanation	PR	Debit	Credit

Part 1 – Classified, multiple-step

Income Statement

Part 2 – Multiple-step

Income Statement

Part 3 – Single-step

Income Statement

*Problem 5-10B

GENERAL JOURNAL   Page_____

Date	Account Titles and Explanation	PR	Debit	Credit

GENERAL JOURNAL

Page____

Date	Account Titles and Explanation	PR	Debit	Credit

GENERAL JOURNAL

Date	Account Titles and Explanation	PR	Debit	Credit

GENERAL JOURNAL

Page____

Date	Account Titles and Explanation	PR	Debit	Credit

1. _____

2. _____

3. _____

4. Multiple-step

Income Statement

5. Single-step

Income Statement

GENERAL JOURNAL

Date	Account Titles and Explanation	PR	Debit	Credit

Part 1

The Online Store
Work Sheet
For Year Ended March 31, 2014

Account Title	Unadjusted Trial Balance Debit	Unadjusted Trial Balance Credit	Adjustments Debit	Adjustments Credit	Income Statement Debit	Income Statement Credit	Balance Sheet and Statement of Changes in Equity Debit	Balance Sheet and Statement of Changes in Equity Credit
Cash	7,000							
Merchandise inventory	39,500							
Supplies	1,600							
Prepaid rent	19,200							
Store equipment	60,000							
Accum. deprec., store equip.		14,000						
Office equipment	23,000							
Accum. deprec., office equip.		6,500						
Accounts payable		16,000						
Lucy Baker, capital		134,600						
Lucy Baker, withdrawals	34,000							
Sales		506,750						
Sales returns and allowances	13,800							
Sales discounts	6,000							
Purchases	346,000							
Purchase returns and allowances		4,600						
Purchase discounts		7,150						
Transportation-in	16,000							
Salaries expenses	58,000							
Rent expense	49,000							
Advertising expense	7,000							
Supplies expense	9,500							
Deprec. exp., store equipment	0							
Deprec. exp., office equipment	0							
Totals	689,600	689,600						

Part 2

GENERAL JOURNAL   Page____

Date	Account Titles and Explanation	PR	Debit	Credit

Part 3

GENERAL LEDGER

Merchandise Inventory   **ACCOUNT NO. 110**

DATE	EXPLANATION	PR	DEBIT	CREDIT	BALANCE

Income Statement

Name _____

GENERAL JOURNAL

Page____

Date	Account Titles and Explanation	PR	Debit	Credit

GENERAL JOURNAL   Page____

Date	Account Titles and Explanation	PR	Debit	Credit

*Problem 5-17B

GENERAL JOURNAL   Page____

Date	Account Titles and Explanation	PR	Debit	Credit

GENERAL JOURNAL

Page____

Date	Account Titles and Explanation	PR	Debit	Credit

GENERAL JOURNAL

Page____

Date	Account Titles and Explanation	PR	Debit	Credit

Part 1   Echo Systems (cont'd.)

GENERAL JOURNAL

Page____

Date	Account Titles and Explanation	PR	Debit	Credit

GENERAL JOURNAL

Date	Account Titles and Explanation	PR	Debit	Credit

Part 1   Echo Systems (cont'd.)

GENERAL JOURNAL   Page____

Date	Account Titles and Explanation	PR	Debit	Credit

GENERAL LEDGER

Cash   ACCOUNT NO. 101

DATE	EXPLANATION	PR	DEBIT	CREDIT	BALANCE
2014 Dec. 31	Beginning Balance				89,090

Part 2   Echo Systems (cont'd.)

Accounts Receivable – Alamo Engineering   ACCOUNT NO. 106.1

DATE	EXPLANATION	PR	DEBIT	CREDIT	BALANCE
2014 Dec. 31	Beginning Balance				-0-

Accounts Receivable – Buckman Services   ACCOUNT NO. 106.2

DATE	EXPLANATION	PR	DEBIT	CREDIT	BALANCE
2014 Dec. 31	Beginning Balance				-0-

Accounts Receivable – Capital Leasing   ACCOUNT NO. 106.3

DATE	EXPLANATION	PR	DEBIT	CREDIT	BALANCE
2014 Dec. 31	Beginning Balance				-0-

Accounts Receivable – Decker Co.   ACCOUNT NO. 106.4

DATE	EXPLANATION	PR	DEBIT	CREDIT	BALANCE
2014 Dec. 31	Beginning Balance				2,700

Accounts Receivable – Elite Corporation   ACCOUNT NO. 106.5

DATE	EXPLANATION	PR	DEBIT	CREDIT	BALANCE
2014 Dec. 31	Beginning Balance				-0-

Accounts Receivable – Fostek Co.   ACCOUNT NO. 106.6

DATE	EXPLANATION	PR	DEBIT	CREDIT	BALANCE
2014 Dec. 31	Beginning Balance				3,000

Accounts Receivable – Grandview Co.   ACCOUNT NO. 106.7

DATE	EXPLANATION	PR	DEBIT	CREDIT	BALANCE
2014 Dec. 31	Beginning Balance				-0-

Accounts Receivable – Hacienda, Inc.   ACCOUNT NO. 106.8

DATE	EXPLANATION	PR	DEBIT	CREDIT	BALANCE
2014 Dec. 31	Beginning Balance				-0-

Accounts Receivable – Images, Inc.   ACCOUNT NO. 106.9

DATE	EXPLANATION	PR	DEBIT	CREDIT	BALANCE
2014 Dec. 31	Beginning Balance				-0-

Part 2   Echo Systems (cont'd.)

Merchandise Inventory   ACCOUNT NO. 119

DATE	EXPLANATION	PR	DEBIT	CREDIT	BALANCE

Computer Supplies   ACCOUNT NO. 126

DATE	EXPLANATION	PR	DEBIT	CREDIT	BALANCE
2014 Dec. 31	Balance				1,440

Prepaid Insurance   ACCOUNT NO. 128

DATE	EXPLANATION	PR	DEBIT	CREDIT	BALANCE
2014 Dec. 31	Beginning Balance				3,240

Prepaid Rent   ACCOUNT NO. 131

DATE	EXPLANATION	PR	DEBIT	CREDIT	BALANCE
2014 Dec. 31	Beginning Balance				2,250

Office Equipment   ACCOUNT NO. 163

DATE	EXPLANATION	PR	DEBIT	CREDIT	BALANCE
2014 Dec. 31	Beginning Balance				18,000

Part 2   Echo Systems (cont'd.)

Accumulated Depreciation, Office Equipment   ACCOUNT NO. 164

DATE	EXPLANATION	PR	DEBIT	CREDIT	BALANCE
2014 Dec. 31	Beginning Balance				1,500

Computer Equipment   ACCOUNT NO. 167

DATE	EXPLANATION	PR	DEBIT	CREDIT	BALANCE
2014 Dec. 31	Beginning Balance				36,000

Accumulated Depreciation, Computer Equipment   ACCOUNT NO. 168

DATE	EXPLANATION	PR	DEBIT	CREDIT	BALANCE
2014 Dec. 31	Beginning Balance				2,250

Accounts Payable   ACCOUNT NO. 201

DATE	EXPLANATION	PR	DEBIT	CREDIT	BALANCE
2014 Dec. 31	Beginning Balance				2,310

Wages Payable   ACCOUNT NO. 210

DATE	EXPLANATION	PR	DEBIT	CREDIT	BALANCE
2014 Dec. 31	Beginning Balance				800

Part 2   Echo Systems (cont'd.)

Unearned Computer Services Revenue   ACCOUNT NO. 236

DATE	EXPLANATION	PR	DEBIT	CREDIT	BALANCE
2014 Dec. 31	Beginning Balance				3,000

Mary Graham, Capital   ACCOUNT NO. 301

DATE	EXPLANATION	PR	DEBIT	CREDIT	BALANCE
2014 Dec. 31	Beginning Balance				145,860

Mary Graham, Withdrawals   ACCOUNT NO. 302

DATE	EXPLANATION	PR	DEBIT	CREDIT	BALANCE

Computer Services Revenue   ACCOUNT NO. 403

DATE	EXPLANATION	PR	DEBIT	CREDIT	BALANCE

Sales   ACCOUNT NO. 413

DATE	EXPLANATION	PR	DEBIT	CREDIT	BALANCE

Sales Discounts   ACCOUNT NO. 414

DATE	EXPLANATION	PR	DEBIT	CREDIT	BALANCE

Sales Returns and Allowances   ACCOUNT NO. 415

DATE	EXPLANATION	PR	DEBIT	CREDIT	BALANCE

Cost of Goods Sold   ACCOUNT NO. 502

DATE	EXPLANATION	PR	DEBIT	CREDIT	BALANCE

Depreciation Expense, Office Equipment   ACCOUNT NO. 612

DATE	EXPLANATION	PR	DEBIT	CREDIT	BALANCE

Depreciation Expense, Computer Equipment   ACCOUNT NO. 613

DATE	EXPLANATION	PR	DEBIT	CREDIT	BALANCE

Wages Expense   ACCOUNT NO. 623

DATE	EXPLANATION	PR	DEBIT	CREDIT	BALANCE

Part 2   Echo Systems (cont'd.)

Insurance Expense   ACCOUNT NO. 637

DATE	EXPLANATION	PR	DEBIT	CREDIT	BALANCE

Rent Expense   ACCOUNT NO. 640

DATE	EXPLANATION	PR	DEBIT	CREDIT	BALANCE

Computer Supplies Expense   ACCOUNT NO. 652

DATE	EXPLANATION	P.R.	DEBIT	CREDIT	BALANCE

Advertising Expense   ACCOUNT NO. 655

DATE	EXPLANATION	PR	DEBIT	CREDIT	BALANCE

Mileage Expense   ACCOUNT NO. 676

DATE	EXPLANATION	PR	DEBIT	CREDIT	BALANCE

Repairs Expense, Computer   ACCOUNT NO. 684

DATE	EXPLANATION	PR	DEBIT	CREDIT	BALANCE

Charitable Donations Expense   ACCOUNT NO. 699

DATE	EXPLANATION	PR	DEBIT	CREDIT	BALANCE

ECHO SYSTEMS
Partial Work Sheet
For Three Months Ended March 31, 2015

Acct. No.	Account Title	Unadjusted Trial Balance Dr.	Cr.	Adjustments Dr.	Cr.	Adjusted Trial Balance Dr.	Cr.
101	Cash						
106.1	Alamo Engineering Co.						
106.2	Buckman Services						
106.3	Capital Leasing						
106.4	Decker Co.						
106.5	Elite Corporation						
106.6	Fostek Co.						
106.7	Grandview Co.						
106.8	Hacienda Inc.						
106.9	Images Inc.						
119	Merchandise inventory						
126	Computer supplies						
128	Prepaid insurance						
131	Prepaid rent						
163	Office equipment						
164	Accum. deprec., office equipment						
167	Computer equipment						
168	Accum. deprec., computer equip.						
201	Accounts payable						
210	Wages payable						
236	Unearned computer services rev.						
301	Mary Graham, capital						
302	Mary Graham, withdrawals						
403	Computer services revenue						
413	Sales						
414	Sales discounts						
415	Sales returns and allowances						
502	Cost of goods sold						
612	Deprec. exp., office equipment						
613	Deprec. exp., computer equip.						
623	Wages expense						
637	Insurance expense						
640	Rent expense						
652	Computer supplies expense						
655	Advertising expense						
676	Mileage expense						
684	Repairs expense, computer						
699	Charitable donations expense						
	Totals						

Part 4   Echo Systems (cont'd.)

ECHO SYSTEMS
Income Statement
For Three Months Ended March 31, 2015

Part 5

ECHO SYSTEMS
Statement of Changes in Equity
For Three Months Ended March 31, 2015

ECHO SYSTEMS
Balance Sheet
March 31, 2015

Part 1   Echo Systems
Journal Entries

GENERAL JOURNAL   Page _____

Date	Account Titles and Explanation	PR	Debit	Credit

Date	Account Titles and Explanation	PR	Debit	Credit

Part 1   Echo Systems (cont'd.)

Date	Account Titles and Explanation	PR	Debit	Credit

Date	Account Titles and Explanation	PR	Debit	Credit

GENERAL LEDGER

Cash   ACCOUNT NO. 101

DATE	EXPLANATION	PR	DEBIT	CREDIT	BALANCE
2014 Dec. 31	Beginning Balance				89,090

Part 2   Echo Systems (cont'd.)

Accounts Receivable – Alamo Engineering   ACCOUNT NO. 106.1

DATE	EXPLANATION	PR	DEBIT	CREDIT	BALANCE
2014 Dec. 31	Beginning Balance				-0-

Accounts Receivable – Buckman Services   ACCOUNT NO. 106.2

DATE	EXPLANATION	PR	DEBIT	CREDIT	BALANCE
2014 Dec. 31	Beginning Balance				-0-

Accounts Receivable – Capital Leasing   ACCOUNT NO. 106.3

DATE	EXPLANATION	PR	DEBIT	CREDIT	BALANCE
2014 Dec. 31	Beginning Balance				-0-

Accounts Receivable – Decker Co.   ACCOUNT NO. 106.4

DATE	EXPLANATION	PR	DEBIT	CREDIT	BALANCE
2014 Dec. 31	Beginning Balance				2,700

Accounts Receivable – Elite Corporation   ACCOUNT NO. 106.5

DATE	EXPLANATION	PR	DEBIT	CREDIT	BALANCE
2014 Dec. 31	Beginning Balance				-0-

Accounts Receivable – Fostek Co.   ACCOUNT NO. 106.6

DATE	EXPLANATION	PR	DEBIT	CREDIT	BALANCE
2014 Dec. 31	Beginning Balance				3,000

Accounts Receivable – Grandview Co.   ACCOUNT NO. 106.7

DATE	EXPLANATION	PR	DEBIT	CREDIT	BALANCE
2014 Dec. 31	Beginning Balance				-0-

Accounts Receivable – Hacienda, Inc.   ACCOUNT NO. 106.8

DATE	EXPLANATION	PR	DEBIT	CREDIT	BALANCE
2014 Dec. 31	Beginning Balance				-0-

Accounts Receivable – Images, Inc.   ACCOUNT NO. 106.9

DATE	EXPLANATION	PR	DEBIT	CREDIT	BALANCE
2014 Dec. 31	Beginning Balance				-0-

Merchandise Inventory   ACCOUNT NO. 119

DATE	EXPLANATION	PR	DEBIT	CREDIT	BALANCE
2014 Dec. 31	Beginning Balance				-0-

Computer Supplies   ACCOUNT NO. 126

DATE	EXPLANATION	PR	DEBIT	CREDIT	BALANCE
2014 Dec. 31	Beginning Balance				1,440

Prepaid Insurance   ACCOUNT NO. 128

DATE	EXPLANATION	PR	DEBIT	CREDIT	BALANCE
2014 Dec. 31	Beginning Balance				3,240

Prepaid Rent   ACCOUNT NO. 131

DATE	EXPLANATION	PR	DEBIT	CREDIT	BALANCE
2014 Dec. 31	Beginning Balance				2,250

Office Equipment   ACCOUNT NO. 163

DATE	EXPLANATION	PR	DEBIT	CREDIT	BALANCE
2014 Dec. 31	Beginning Balance				18,000

Accumulated Depreciation, Office Equipment   ACCOUNT NO. 164

DATE	EXPLANATION	PR	DEBIT	CREDIT	BALANCE
2014 Dec. 31	Beginning Balance				1,500

Computer Equipment   ACCOUNT NO. 167

DATE	EXPLANATION	PR	DEBIT	CREDIT	BALANCE
2014 Dec. 31	Beginning Balance				36,000

Accumulated Depreciation, Computer Equipment   ACCOUNT NO. 168

DATE	EXPLANATION	PR	DEBIT	CREDIT	BALANCE
2014 Dec. 31	Beginning Balance				2,250

Part 2   Echo Systems (cont'd.)

Accounts Payable   ACCOUNT NO. 201

DATE	EXPLANATION	PR	DEBIT	CREDIT	BALANCE
2014 Dec. 31	Beginning Balance				2,310

Wages Payable   ACCOUNT NO. 210

DATE	EXPLANATION	PR	DEBIT	CREDIT	BALANCE
2014 Dec. 31	Beginning Balance				800

Unearned Computer Services Revenue   ACCOUNT NO. 236

DATE	EXPLANATION	PR	DEBIT	CREDIT	BALANCE
2014 Dec. 31	Beginning Balance				3,000

Mary Graham, Capital   ACCOUNT NO. 301

DATE	EXPLANATION	PR	DEBIT	CREDIT	BALANCE
2014 Dec. 31	Beginning Balance				145,860

Mary Graham, Withdrawals   ACCOUNT NO. 302

DATE	EXPLANATION	PR	DEBIT	CREDIT	BALANCE

Computer Services Revenue   ACCOUNT NO. 403

DATE	EXPLANATION	PR	DEBIT	CREDIT	BALANCE

Sales   ACCOUNT NO. 413

DATE	EXPLANATION	PR	DEBIT	CREDIT	BALANCE

Sales Discounts   ACCOUNT NO. 414

DATE	EXPLANATION	PR	DEBIT	CREDIT	BALANCE

Sales Returns and Allowances   ACCOUNT NO. 415

DATE	EXPLANATION	PR	DEBIT	CREDIT	BALANCE

Purchases   ACCOUNT NO. 505

DATE	EXPLANATION	PR	DEBIT	CREDIT	BALANCE

Part 2   Echo Systems (cont'd.)

Purchase Returns and Allowances   ACCOUNT NO. 506

DATE	EXPLANATION	PR	DEBIT	CREDIT	BALANCE

Purchase Discounts   ACCOUNT NO.507

DATE	EXPLANATION	PR	DEBIT	CREDIT	BALANCE

Transportation-In   ACCOUNT NO. 508

DATE	EXPLANATION	PR	DEBIT	CREDIT	BALANCE

Depreciation Expense, Office Equipment   ACCOUNT NO. 612

DATE	EXPLANATION	PR	DEBIT	CREDIT	BALANCE

Depreciation Expense, Computer Equipment   ACCOUNT NO. 613

DATE	EXPLANATION	PR	DEBIT	CREDIT	BALANCE

Wages Expense   ACCOUNT NO. 623

DATE	EXPLANATION	PR	DEBIT	CREDIT	BALANCE

Insurance Expense   ACCOUNT NO. 637

DATE	EXPLANATION	PR	DEBIT	CREDIT	BALANCE

Rent Expense   ACCOUNT NO. 640

DATE	EXPLANATION	PR	DEBIT	CREDIT	BALANCE

Computer Supplies Expense   ACCOUNT NO. 652

DATE	EXPLANATION	P.R.	DEBIT	CREDIT	BALANCE

Advertising Expense   ACCOUNT NO. 655

DATE	EXPLANATION	PR	DEBIT	CREDIT	BALANCE

Mileage Expense   ACCOUNT NO. 676

DATE	EXPLANATION	PR	DEBIT	CREDIT	BALANCE

Repairs Expense, Computer   ACCOUNT NO. 684

DATE	EXPLANATION	PR	DEBIT	CREDIT	BALANCE

Charitable Donations Expense   ACCOUNT NO. 699

DATE	EXPLANATION	PR	DEBIT	CREDIT	BALANCE

Part 3   Echo Systems (concl'd.)

ECHO SYSTEMS
Partial Work Sheet
March 31, 2015

Acct. No.	Account Title	Unadjusted Trial Balance		Adjustments		Adjusted Trial Balance	
		Debit	Credit	Debit	Credit	Debit	Credit
101	Cash						
106.1	Alamo Engineering Co.						
106.2	Buckman Services						
106.3	Capital Leasing						
106.4	Decker Co.						
106.5	Elite Corporation						
106.6	Fostek Co.						
106.7	Grandview Co.						
106.8	Hacienda Inc.						
106.9	Images Inc.						
119	Merchandise inventory						
126	Computer supplies						
128	Prepaid Insurance						
131	Prepaid rent						
163	Office equipment						
164	Accum. deprec., office equipment						
167	Computer equipment						
168	Accum. deprec., computer equip.						
201	Accounts payable						
210	Wages payable						
236	Unearned computer services rev.						
301	Mary Graham, capital						
302	Mary Graham, withdrawals						
403	Computer services revenue						
413	Sales						
414	Sales discounts						
415	Sales returns and allowances						
505	Purchases						
506	Purchase returns and allowances						
507	Purchase discounts						
508	Transportation-in						
612	Deprec. exp., office equipment						
613	Deprec. exp., computer equip.						
623	Wages expense						
637	Insurance expense						
640	Rent expense						
652	Computer supplies expense						
655	Advertising expense						
676	Mileage expense						
684	Repairs expense, computer						
699	Charitable donations expense						
	Totals						

Parts 4, 5, and 6: Use the forms provided earlier.

1. _____
_____
_____

2. _____
_____
_____

Quick Study 6-2

1500 − 30 + 250 + 70 = 1790 units in ending inventory

Quick Study 6-3

3000 + 150 (Transportation − In)
+ 200 (Import duties)
+ 50 (Insurance)
= 3400

Quick Study 6-4

37,500 + 1,200 (Transportation − In)
+ 490 (Cleaning Expenses)
+ 150 (Insurance)

= 39,340

Quick Study 6-5

10 units @ $50 = 500 (Beginning Inventory)
10 units @ $51 = 510 (1st week purchase)
10 units @ $52 = 520 (2nd week purchase)
10 units @ $55 = 550 (3rd week purchase)
10 units @ $60 = 600 (4th week purchase)

Units Available = 50 units

Cost of Goods Available for Sale = 2,680

a. FIFO Perpetual

Date	Purchases	Sales (at cost)	Inventory Balance
Jan 1	310 – 3.00 = 930.00		310 – 3.00 = 930.00
9)	75 – 3.20 = 240.00		310 – 3.00 = 930.00
			75 – 3.20 = 240.00
25)	100 – 3.35 = 335.00		310 – 3.00 = 930.00
			75 – 3.20 = 240.00
			100 – 3.35 = 335.00
28		310 – 3.00 = 930.00	
		35 – 3.20 = 112.00	
Total	1505.00	1042.00	463.00

b. Moving Weighted Average Perpetual

Date	Purchases	Sales (at cost)	Inventory Balance

Date	Purchases	Sales (at cost)	Inventory Balance

Quick Study 6-8

Date	Purchases/ Transportation-In/ (Purchase Returns/Discounts)			Cost of Goods Sold/ (Returns to Inventory)			Balance in Inventory		
	Units	Cost Per Unit	Total $	Units	Cost Per Unit	Total $	Units	Avg Cost Per Unit	Total $
Jan. 1		BFWD					10	$15.00	$150.00
3				6					
7	25	$18.50	$462.50						
8			50.00						
17			(46.25)						
18				14					

Calculations:

_____
_____
_____
_____
_____
_____
_____

Quick Study 6-9

a. _____
b. _____
c. _____

Parts a and b

Inventory Items	Units on Hand	Per Unit Cost	Per Unit NRV	Total Cost	Total NRV	LCNRV applied to: a. Inventory as a Group	b. Each Product
Aprons	9	$6.00	$5.50				
Bottles	12	3.50	4.25				
Candles	25	8.00	7.00				

Part c   GENERAL JOURNAL   Page____

Date	Account Titles and Explanation	PR	Debit	Credit

Quick Study 6-11

a. _____
b. _____
c. _____
d. _____
e. _____
f. _____

Quick Study 6-12

_____
_____
_____
_____
_____
_____
_____
_____
_____
_____
_____
_____
_____
_____
_____

a. _____

_____

_____

_____

_____

_____

_____

_____

_____

b. _____

Quick Study 6-14

_____

_____

_____

_____

_____

_____

_____

_____

_____

_____

Quick Study 6-15

_____

_____

_____

_____

_____

_____

_____

_____

_____

_____

_____

_____

_____

_____

Chapter 6   *Quick Study 6-16   Name _____

a. _____
_____
_____

b. _____
_____
_____

*Quick Study 6-17

_____
_____
_____
_____
_____
_____

*Quick Study 6-18

a. Days' sales in inventory: _____
_____
_____
_____
_____
_____

b. Merchandise turnover: _____
_____
_____
_____
_____
_____

Chapter 6   Exercise 6-1   *Name* _____

a. FIFO Perpetual

Date	Purchases	Sales (at cost)	Inventory Balance

Gross profit calculation under FIFO:

b. Moving weighted Average Perpetual

Date	Purchases	Sales (at cost)	Inventory Balance

Gross Profit Calculation under Moving Weighted Average:

_____
_____
_____
_____
_____
_____

Exercise 6-2

Specific Identification

Date	Purchases	Sales (at cost)	Inventory Balance

Gross Profit Calculation under Specific Identification:

_____
_____
_____
_____
_____
_____

1.

2.

3(a). FIFO perpetual

Date	Purchases	Sales (at cost)	Inventory Balance

3(b). Moving weighted-average perpetual

Date	Purchases	Sales (at cost)	Inventory Balance

Exercise 6-4

Specific Identification

Date	Purchases	Sales (at cost)	Inventory Balance

Trout Company			
Income Statements			
For the Year Ended December 31, 2014			
	FIFO	Moving Weighted Average	Specific Identification

1. _____

2. _____

Exercise 6-6

Date	Purchases/ Transportation-In/ (Purchase Returns/Discounts)			Cost of Goods Sold/ (Returns to Inventory)			Balance in Inventory		
	Units	Cost Per Unit	Total $	Units	Cost Per Unit	Total $	Units	Avg Cost Per Unit	Total $
Mar. 1		BFWD					60	$94.00	$5,640.00
2	35	$96.00							
3				22					
4				(2)					
7				65					
17	40	97.00							
28				43					
Totals									

Calculations:

_____
_____
_____
_____
_____

Analysis component:

_____
_____
_____

Parts a and b

Inventory Items	Units on Hand	Per Unit Cost	Per Unit NRV	Total Cost	Total NRV	LCNRV applied to: a. Inventory as a Group	LCNRV applied to: b. Each Product
BB	22	$110	$115				
FM	15	145	138				
MB	36	186	172				
SL	40	78	92				

Part c   **GENERAL JOURNAL**   Page____

Date	Account Titles and Explanation	PR	Debit	Credit

1. _____

_____

_____

2.

	For years ended December 31, 2014, 2015, and 2016 Income statement information should have been reported as:	Income statement information actually reported for years ended December 31,		
		2014	2015	2016
Sales				
Cost of goods sold:				
Beginning inventory				
+ Purchases				
- Ending inventory				
= Cost of goods sold				
Gross profit				

_____
_____
_____
_____
_____
_____
_____
_____
_____
_____
_____

Exercise 6-10

	At Cost	*At Retail*

Exercise 6-11

a. Estimated cost of physical inventory: _____

_____

b. Shrinkage at cost and at retail:	**At Cost**	**At Retail**

	Ending Inventory	Cost of Goods Sold
a. FIFO periodic:		

_____

_____

_____

_____

| **b. Weighted-average cost periodic:** | | |

_____

_____

_____

_____

Which method provides the lower net income and why?

_____

_____

_____

*Exercise 6-13

	Ending Inventory	Cost of Goods Sold
a. FIFO periodic:		

_____

_____

_____

_____

| **b. Weighted-average cost periodic:** | | |

_____

_____

_____

_____

Which method provides the lower net income and why?

_____

_____

_____

*Exercise 6-15

Merchandise turnover (2015):

Merchandise turnover (2014):

Days' sales in inventory (2015):

Days' sales in inventory (2014):

Comment on Russo's efficiency in using its assets to support increasing sales from 2014 to 2015.

Chapter 6   Problem 6-1A   *Name* _____

1a. FIFO Perpetual

Date	Purchases	Sales (at cost)	Inventory Balance

1b. Moving Weighted-Average Perpetual

Date	Purchases	Cost of Goods Sold	Inventory Balance

2. Specific Identification

Date	Purchases	Cost of Goods Sold	Inventory Balance

3.

GENERAL JOURNAL

Page_____

Date	Account Titles and Explanation	PR	Debit	Credit
a.				
b.				

GENERAL JOURNAL   Page____

Date	Account Titles and Explanation	PR	Debit	Credit
c.				

Chapter 6   *Problem 6-2A   *Name* _____

a. FIFO basis:

_____
_____
_____
_____
_____
_____
_____

b. Weighted Average basis:

_____
_____
_____
_____
_____
_____
_____

Problem 6-3A

Calculation of cost of goods available for sale and units available for sale:

_____
_____
_____
_____
_____
_____
_____
_____
_____

Calculation of units in ending inventory:

_____
_____
_____
_____
_____
_____

1a. FIFO Perpetual

Date	Purchases	Cost of Goods Sold	Inventory Balance

1b. Moving Weighted-Average Perpetual

Date	Purchases	Cost of Goods Sold	Inventory Balance

2.

	FIFO	Moving Weighted Average
Sales		
Cost of goods sold................		
Gross profit		

Analysis component: _____

_____

_____

_____

_____

_____

*Problem 6-4A

a. FIFO basis:

_____

_____

_____

_____

_____

_____

_____

_____

b. Weighted Average basis:

_____

_____

_____

_____

_____

_____

_____

_____

Fresh Express Company
Income Statement Comparing FIFO and Moving Weighted Average Cost
For Year Ended December 31, 2014

	FIFO	Moving Weighted Average
Sales		
Cost of goods sold		
Gross profit		
Operating expenses		
Net income		

Supporting calculations:

_____

_____

_____

_____

_____

_____

_____

_____

_____

_____

_____

_____

a. FIFO Perpetual

Date	Purchases	Cost of Goods Sold	Inventory Balance

b. Moving Weighted-Average Perpetual

Date	Purchases	Cost of Goods Sold	Inventory Balance

Analysis component:

_____
_____
_____
_____
_____
_____
_____

*Problem 6-6A

	FIFO	Weighted Average
Fresh Express Company		
Income Statement Comparing FIFO and Weighted Average Periodic		
For Year Ended December 31, 2014		
	FIFO	**Weighted Average**
Sales		
Cost of goods sold		
Gross profit		
Operating expenses		
Net income		

Supporting calculations:

_____
_____
_____
_____
_____
_____
_____
_____
_____
_____
_____
_____
_____

Part 1

a. Cost of Goods Sold:		*2014*	*2015*	*2016*
Reported.............................		_____	_____	_____
Adjustments:	12/31/2014 error	_____	_____	_____
	12/31/2015 error	_____	_____	_____
Corrected.............................		_____	_____	_____

b. Net Income:		*2014*	*2015*	*2016*
Reported.............................		_____	_____	_____
Adjustments:	12/31/2014 error	_____	_____	_____
	12/31/2015 error	_____	_____	_____
Corrected.............................		_____	_____	_____

c. Total Current Assets:		*2014*	*2015*	*2016*
Reported.............................		_____	_____	_____
Adjustments:	12/31/2014 error	_____	_____	_____
	12/31/2015 error	_____	_____	_____
Corrected.............................		_____	_____	_____

d. Equity:		*2014*	*2015*	*2016*
Reported.............................		_____	_____	_____
Adjustments:	12/31/2014 error	_____	_____	_____
	12/31/2015 error	_____	_____	_____
Corrected.............................		_____	_____	_____

Analysis component:

_____

_____

_____

_____

_____

_____

_____

_____

_____

_____

_____

_____

_____

_____

_____

Chapter 6   Problem 6-8A   *Name* _____

	2014	2015	2016
Corrected Ending Inventory			
Corrected Cost of Goods Sold			
Corrected Net Income			

Problem 6-9A

| | Units on Hand | Per Unit | | Total Cost | Total NRV | LCNRV applied to: | |
		Cost	NRV			a. Major Group	b. Separately to Each Product
Inventory Items							
Audio equip:							
Receivers	335	$185	$ 196				
MP3 players	250	220	200				
Mixers	316	174	190				
Stands	194	100	82				
Video:							
Televisions	470	295	250				
Video cards	281	180	168				
Video recorders	202	615	644				
Car Audio:							
GPS navigators	175	142	168				
Receivers	160	195	210				

2a.   GENERAL JOURNAL   Page____

Date		Account Titles and Explanation	PR	Debit	Credit

2b.   GENERAL JOURNAL   Page____

Date		Account Titles and Explanation	PR	Debit	Credit

Problem 6-10A

Part 1

Earthly Goods
Estimated Inventory
December 31, 2014

	At Cost	*At Retail*

Part 2

Earthly Goods
Inventory Shortage
December 31, 2014

	At Cost	*At Retail*

Chapter 6   Problem 6-13A   *Name* _____

Part 1

	At Cost	At Retail

Part 2

*Problem 6-14A

Part 1

Part 2

a. FIFO basis:

_____

_____

_____

_____

_____

_____

b. Weighted Average basis:

_____

_____

_____

_____

_____

_____

_____

Chapter 6   Problem 6-1B   *Name* _____

1a. FIFO Perpetual

Date	Purchases	Sales (at cost)	Inventory Balance

1b. Moving Weighted-Average Perpetual

Date	Purchases	Sales (at cost)	Inventory Balance

2. Specific Identification

Date	Purchases	Cost of Goods Sold	Inventory Balance

3.   **GENERAL JOURNAL**   Page____

Date	Account Titles and Explanation	PR	Debit	Credit
a.				
b.				
c.				

a. FIFO basis:

_____
_____
_____
_____
_____
_____

b. Weighted Average basis:

_____
_____
_____
_____
_____
_____

1a. FIFO Perpetual

Date	Purchases	Cost of Goods Sold	Inventory Balance

1b. Moving Weighted-Average Perpetual

Date	Purchases	Cost of Goods Sold	Inventory Balance

2.

	FIFO	Moving Weighted Average
Sales		
Cost of goods sold................		
Gross profit		

Analysis component: _____

_____

_____

_____

_____

*Problem 6-4B

a. FIFO basis:

_____

_____

_____

_____

_____

c. Weighted Average basis:

_____

_____

_____

_____

_____

_____

_____

Blizzard Company
Income Statement Comparing FIFO and Moving Weighted Average Cost
For Year Ended December 31, 2014

	FIFO	Moving Weighted Average
Sales		
Cost of goods sold		
Gross profit		
Operating expenses		
Net income		

Supporting calculations:

_____
_____
_____
_____
_____
_____
_____
_____
_____
_____
_____
_____
_____

a. FIFO Perpetual

Date	Purchases	Cost of Goods Sold	Inventory Balance

b. Moving Weighted-Average Perpetual

Date	Purchases	Cost of Goods Sold	Inventory Balance

Analysis component:

_____
_____
_____
_____
_____
_____
_____
_____
_____

Blizzard Company
Income Statement Comparing FIFO and Weighted Average Periodic
For Year Ended December 31, 2014

	FIFO	Weighted Average
Sales		
Cost of goods sold		
Gross profit		
Operating expenses		
Net income		

Supporting calculations:

_____
_____
_____
_____
_____
_____
_____
_____
_____
_____

a. FIFO Periodic

_____
_____
_____
_____
_____
_____
_____
_____

b. Weighted Average Periodic

_____
_____
_____
_____
_____
_____
_____
_____

Part 1

a. Cost of Goods Sold:	*2014*	*2015*	*2016*
Reported..	_____	_____	_____
Adjustments: 12/31/2014 error	_____	_____	_____
12/31/2015 error	_____	_____	_____
Corrected..	_____	_____	_____

b. Net Income:	*2014*	*2015*	*2016*
Reported..	_____	_____	_____
Adjustments: 12/31/2014 error	_____	_____	_____
12/31/2015 error	_____	_____	_____
Corrected..	_____	_____	_____

c. Total Current Assets:	*2014*	*2015*	*2016*
Reported..	_____	_____	_____
Adjustments: 12/31/2014 error	_____	_____	_____
12/31/2015 error	_____	_____	_____
Corrected..	_____	_____	_____

d. Equity:	*2014*	*2015*	*2016*
Reported..	_____	_____	_____
Adjustments: 12/31/2014 error	_____	_____	_____
12/31/2015 error	_____	_____	_____
Corrected..	_____	_____	_____

Analysis component:

_____
_____
_____
_____
_____
_____
_____
_____
_____
_____
_____
_____
_____
_____
_____

Part 1

	Incorrect Income Statement Information For Years Ended December 31				Corrected Income Statement Information For Years Ended December 31			
	2014	%	2015	%	2014	%	2015	%
Sales								
Cost of goods sold ...								
Gross profit								

Part 2 _____

_____
_____
_____
_____

Problem 6-9B

Inventory Items	Per Unit			Total Cost	Total NRV	LCNRV applied to:	
	Units on Hand	Cost	NRV			a. Major Category	b. Separately to Each Product
Office furniture:							
Desks	430	$261	$305				
Credenzas	290	227	256				
Chairs	585	49	43				
Bookshelves	320	93	82				
Filing cabinets:							
Two-drawer	215	81	70				
Four-drawer	400	135	122				
Lateral	178	104	118				
Office Equip.:							
Fax machines	415	168	200				
Copiers	544	317	288				
Typewriters	355	125	117				

2a.   GENERAL JOURNAL   Page____

Date	Account Titles and Explanation	PR	Debit	Credit

2b.   GENERAL JOURNAL   Page____

Date	Account Titles and Explanation	PR	Debit	Credit

Problem 6-10B

_____

_____

_____

_____

_____

_____

_____

_____

_____

_____

_____

_____

_____

_____

_____

_____

_____

_____

Part 1

THE WILKE CO.
Estimated Inventory
December 31, 2014

	At Cost	At Retail

Part 2

THE WILKE CO.
Inventory Shortage
December 31, 2014

	At Cost	At Retail

Part 1

	At Cost	At Retail

*Problem 6-14B   Part 1

Part 2
a. FIFO basis:

b. Weighted Average basis:

1. P
2. AR
3. AR
4. AP

Quick Study 7-2

1. I
2. I
3. O
4. O
5. I
6. O
7. O
8. I

Quick Study 7-3

a. Sale Journal
b. Purchases Journal
c. Cash Disbursements Journal
d. Cash Disbursements Journal
e. Purchases Journal
f. Cash Receipts Journal
g. Cash Receipts Journal

Quick Study 7-4

GENERAL JOURNAL   Page____

Date	Account Titles and Explanation	PR	Debit	Credit
Nov 12	Automobiles		15,000	
	Capital			15,000
	owner contributed automobiles			
Nov 19	Sales Returns and Allowances		150	
	Accounts Receivable			150
	Returned merchandise			
Nov 19	Merchandise Inventory		95	
	Cost of goods sold			95
	returned to inventory			
Nov 28	Account Payable		170	
	Merchandise Inventory			170
	Defective merchandise			

1. DR   5. NE
2. NE   6. CR
3. NE   7. NE
4. CR

Quick Study 7-6

1. CR   5. DR
2. NE   6. DR
3. CR   7. NE
4. NE

Quick Study 7-7

Sales Journal					Page
Mar Date	Account Debited	Invoice Number	PR	Accounts Receivable Dr. Sales Cr.	Cost of Goods Sold Dr. Merchandise Inventory Cr.
3	Tim Edson	1103		3,000	2040
10	Willis Com	1104		10,800	7344
11	Ellton K	1105		7400	5032
	Total			21,200	14,416

Quick Study 7-8

Cash Receipts Journal									Page
Mar Date	Account Credited	PR	Explanation	Cash Dr.	Sales Disc. Dr.	Accts. Rec. Cr.	Sales Cr.	Other Accts. Cr.	COGS Dr. Merch. Inv. Cr.
18	Tim Edson		Invoice 1103	2940	60	3000			
30	Willis C		Invoice 1104	10 800		10800			
31	Sales		Cash sale	6200			6200		4216
	Totals			19,940	60	13800	6200		4216

Quick Study 7-9

Purchases Journal								Page
Mar Date	Account Credited	Date of Invoice	Terms	PR	Accounts Payable Cr.	Merch. Inventory Dr.	Office Supplies Dr.	Other Accounts Dr.
2	Tex Com	Mar 2	3/10, n/20		4800	4800		
12	Littleton	12	2/15, n/30		14000	14000		
13	W C	13	2/15 n/45		9400			9400
	Total				28200	18800		9400

Cash Disbursements Journal								Page
Mar Date	Ch. No.	Payee	Account Debited	PR	Cash Cr.	Merch. Inventory Cr.	Other Accounts Dr.	Accounts Payable Dr.
14	101	Tex C	Tex C		4800			4800
27	102	Littleton	Littleton		13720	280		14000
31	103	Thorn	Rent E		6500		6500	
		Total			25020	280	6500	18,800

Exercise 7-1

Sales Journal						Page
Date	Account Debited	Invoice Number	PR	Accounts Receivable Dr. Sales Cr.	Cost of Goods Sold Dr. Merchandise Inventory Cr.	

*Exercise 7-2

Sales Journal				Page
Date	Account Debited	Invoice No.	PR	Accounts Receivable Dr. Sales Cr.

Exercise 7-3

Cash Receipts Journal									Page
Date	Account Credited	PR	Explanation	Cash Dr.	Sales Disc. Dr.	Accts. Rec. Cr.	Sales Cr.	Other Accts. Cr.	COGS Dr. Merch. Inv. Cr.

Cash Receipts Journal								Page
Date	Account Credited	PR	Explanation	Cash Dr.	Sales Disc. Dr.	Accts. Rec. Cr.	Sales Cr.	Other Accts. Cr.

Exercise 7-5

Purchases Journal								Page
Date	Account Credited	Date of Invoice	Terms	PR	Accounts Payable Cr.	Merch. Inventory Dr.	Office Supplies Dr.	Other Accounts Dr.

*Exercise 7-6

Purchases Journal								Page
Date	Account Credited	Date of Invoice	Terms	PR	Accts. Payable Cr.	Purchases Dr.	Office Supplies Dr.	Other Accts. Dr.

Exercise 7-7

Cash Disbursements Journal								Page
Date	Ch. No.	Payee	Account Debited	PR	Cash Cr.	Merch. Inventory Cr.	Other Accounts Dr.	Accounts Payable Dr.

Cash Disbursements Journal								Page
Date	Ch. No.	Payee	Account Debited	PR	Cash Cr.	Purch. Disc. Cr.	Other Accounts Dr.	Accts. Payable Dr.

Exercise 7-9

Part 1 – Wilson Purchasing

Purchases Journal								Page
Date	Account Credited	Date of Invoice	Terms	PR	Accounts Payable Cr.	Merch. Inventory Dr.	Office Supplies Dr.	Other Accounts Dr.

Cash Disbursements Journal								Page
Date	Ch. No.	Payee	Account Debited	PR	Cash Cr.	Merch. Inventory Cr.	Other Accounts Dr.	Accounts Payable Dr.

GENERAL JOURNAL   Page____

Date	Account Titles and Explanation	PR	Debit	Credit

Part 2 – Hostel Sales

				Sales Journal		Page
Date	Account Debited	Invoice Number	PR	Accounts Receivable Dr. Sales Cr.		Cost of Goods Sold Dr. Merchandise Inventory Cr.

				Cash Receipts Journal						Page
Date	Account Credited	PR	Explanation	Cash Dr.	Sales Disc. Dr.	Accts. Rec. Cr.	Sales Cr.	Other Accts. Cr.	COGS Dr. Merch. Inv. Cr.	

GENERAL JOURNAL   Page____

Date	Account Titles and Explanation	PR	Debit	Credit

*Exercise 7-10

Part 1 – Wilson Purchasing

					Purchases Journal			Page
Date	Account Credited	Date of Invoice	Terms	PR	Accts. Payable Cr.	Purchases Dr.	Office Supplies Dr.	Other Accts. Dr.

Cash Disbursements Journal								Page
Date	Ch. No.	Payee	Account Debited	PR	Cash Cr.	Purch. Disc. Cr.	Other Accounts Dr.	Accts. Payable Dr.

GENERAL JOURNAL   Page____

Date	Account Titles and Explanation	PR	Debit	Credit

Part 2 – Hostel Sales

Sales Journal				Page
Date	Account Debited	Invoice No.	PR	Accounts Receivable Dr. Sales Cr.

Cash Receipts Journal								Page
Date	Account Credited	PR	Explanation	Cash Dr.	Sales Disc. Dr.	Accts. Rec. Cr.	Sales Cr.	Other Accts. Cr.

GENERAL JOURNAL   Page____

Date	Account Titles and Explanation	PR	Debit	Credit

_____
_____
_____
_____
_____
_____
_____
_____
_____
_____
_____
_____
_____

Exercise 7-12

a. _____

b. _____

c. _____

d. _____

e. _____

Exercise 7-13

Part 1   ACCOUNTS RECEIVABLE SUBLEDGER

Sanders Farrell	Don Holland	Brad Smithers

Part 2   GENERAL LEDGER

Accounts Receivable	Sales	Sales Returns and Allowances

Part 3

Schedule of Accounts Receivable

*Exercise 7-14

Parts 1 and 2

GENERAL LEDGER

Cash	Accounts Payable	Sales Discounts

Accts. Receivable	Notes Payable	Purchases

Prepaid Insurance	Sales	Purchase Returns and Allowances

Store Equipment	Sales Returns and Allowances	Purchase Discounts

ACCOUNTS RECEIVABLE SUBLEDGER

Jack Hertz	Trudy Stone	Dave Waylon

ACCOUNTS PAYABLE SUBLEDGER

Grass Corp.	McGrew Company	Sulter Inc.

Special Journal		Subledger	
Sales	S	Accounts Receivable	AR
Purchases...................	P	Accounts Payable	AP
Cash Receipts	CR	Merchandise Inventory .	MI
Cash Disbursements ..	CD	No Effect........................	NE
General Journal...........	G		

Date	Transaction	Special Journal	Subledger
Mar. 1	*Sold merchandise on credit.*	*S*	*AR/MI*
2	Defective merchandise sold on March 1 was returned by the customer. It was scrapped.		
3	Purchased office equipment on credit; terms n/30.		
5	Received payment regarding the March 1 sale.		
10	Received a credit memorandum from the supplier regarding defective equipment purchased on March 3.		
14	Sold merchandise for cash.		
16	Purchased merchandise inventory on credit; terms 1/5, n30.		
17	Paid the balance owing regarding the March 3 transaction.		
18	Purchased merchandise inventory for cash.		
21	Paid for the merchandise purchased on March 16.		
22	Sold old equipment for cash.		
30	Paid salaries for the month of March.		
30	Accrued utilities for the month of March.		
30	Closed the credit balance in the income summary to Capital.		

Sales Journal					Page 3
Date	Account Debited	Invoice Number	PR	Accounts Receivable Dr. Sales Cr.	Cost of Goods Sold Dr. Merchandise Inventory Cr.

Cash Receipts Journal									Page 3
Date	Account Credited	PR	Explanation	Cash Dr.	Sales Disc. Dr.	Accts. Rec. Cr.	Sales Cr.	Other Accts. Cr.	COGS Dr. Merch. Inv. Cr.

Purchases Journal								Page 3
Date	Account	Date of Invoice	Terms	PR	Accounts Payable Cr.	Merch. Inventory Dr.	Office Supplies Dr.	Other Accounts Dr.

Cash Disbursements Journal								Page 3
Date	Ch. No.	Payee	Account Debited	PR	Cash Cr.	Merch. Inventory Cr.	Other Accounts Dr.	Accounts Payable Dr.

GENERAL JOURNAL   Page____

Date	Account Titles and Explanation	PR	Debit	Credit

Problem 7-3A   Part 1

ACCOUNTS RECEIVABLE SUBLEDGER

Paul Abrams   ACCOUNT NO. 106-1

DATE	EXPLANATION	PR	DEBIT	CREDIT	BALANCE

Linda Hobart   ACCOUNT NO. 106-2

DATE	EXPLANATION	PR	DEBIT	CREDIT	BALANCE

Kelly Schaefer   ACCOUNT NO. 106-3

DATE	EXPLANATION	PR	DEBIT	CREDIT	BALANCE

Part 2   ACCOUNTS PAYABLE SUBLEDGER

Frank's Supply   ACCOUNT NO. 201-1

DATE	EXPLANATION	PR	DEBIT	CREDIT	BALANCE

Baskin Company   ACCOUNT NO. 201-2

DATE	EXPLANATION	PR	DEBIT	CREDIT	BALANCE

Sprocket Company   ACCOUNT NO. 201-3

DATE	EXPLANATION	PR	DEBIT	CREDIT	BALANCE

Eau Claire Inc.   ACCOUNT NO. 201-4

DATE	EXPLANATION	PR	DEBIT	CREDIT	BALANCE

Part 3

Sales Journal					Page 3
Date	Account Debited	Invoice Number	PR	Accounts Receivable Dr. Sales Cr.	Cost of Goods Sold Dr. Merchandise Inventory Cr.

Cash Receipts Journal									Page 3
Date	Accounts Credited	PR	Explanation	Cash Dr.	Sales Disc. Dr.	Accts. Rec. Cr.	Sales Cr.	Other Accts. Cr.	COGS Dr. Merch. Inv. Cr.

Purchases Journal   Page 3

Date	Account Credited	Date of Invoice	Terms	PR	Accounts Payable Cr.	Merch. Inventory Dr.	Office Supplies Dr.	Other Accounts Dr.

Cash Disbursements Journal   Page 3

Date	Ch. No.	Payee	Account Debited	PR	Cash Cr.	Merch. Inventory Cr.	Other Accounts Dr.	Accounts Payable Dr.

GENERAL JOURNAL   Page____

Date	Account Titles and Explanation	PR	Debit	Credit

GENERAL LEDGER

Cash   ACCOUNT NO. 101

DATE	EXPLANATION	PR	DEBIT	CREDIT	BALANCE
2014					
Mar. 31	Balance brought forward				167,000

Accounts Receivable   ACCOUNT NO. 106

DATE	EXPLANATION	PR	DEBIT	CREDIT	BALANCE

Merchandise Inventory   ACCOUNT NO. 119

DATE	EXPLANATION	PR	DEBIT	CREDIT	BALANCE
2014					
Mar. 31	Balance brought forward				105,000

Office Supplies   ACCOUNT NO. 124

DATE	EXPLANATION	PR	DEBIT	CREDIT	BALANCE

Store Supplies   ACCOUNT NO. 125

DATE	EXPLANATION	PR	DEBIT	CREDIT	BALANCE

Store Equipment   ACCOUNT NO. 165

DATE	EXPLANATION	PR	DEBIT	CREDIT	BALANCE

Accounts Payable ACCOUNT NO. 201

DATE	EXPLANATION	PR	DEBIT	CREDIT	BALANCE

Long-Term Notes Payable ACCOUNT NO. 251

DATE	EXPLANATION	PR	DEBIT	CREDIT	BALANCE
2014					
Mar. 31	Balance brought forward				167,000

Jeff Newton, Capital ACCOUNT NO. 301

DATE	EXPLANATION	PR	DEBIT	CREDIT	BALANCE
2014					
Mar. 31	Balance brought forward				105,000

Sales ACCOUNT NO. 413

DATE	EXPLANATION	PR	DEBIT	CREDIT	BALANCE

Sales Discounts ACCOUNT NO. 415

DATE	EXPLANATION	PR	DEBIT	CREDIT	BALANCE

Cost of Goods Sold ACCOUNT NO. 502

DATE	EXPLANATION	PR	DEBIT	CREDIT	BALANCE

Sales Salaries Expense ACCOUNT NO. 621

DATE	EXPLANATION	PR	DEBIT	CREDIT	BALANCE

Advertising Expense   ACCOUNT NO. 655

DATE	EXPLANATION	PR	DEBIT	CREDIT	BALANCE

NOTE: For Parts 2 and 3, journalizing and posting, continue journalizing the transactions in the journals provided in Problem 7-3A.

Part 5

Trial Balance

	Debit	Credit

Schedule of Accounts Receivable

Schedule of Accounts Payable

Analysis component:

Parts 1, 2, 3

Sales Journal					Page 3
Date	Account Debited	Invoice Number	PR	Accounts Receivable Dr. Sales Cr.	Cost of Goods Sold Dr. Merchandise Inventory Cr.
2014					
Oct. 6	M. Craig	913	√	3,300	1,600
12	V. Foresman	914	√	3,650	1,900
15	A. Ihrig	915	√	3,100	1,700

Purchases Journal								Page 2
Date	Account	Date of Invoice	Terms	PR	Accounts Payable Cr.	Merch. Inventory Dr.	Office Supplies Dr.	Other Accounts Dr.
2014								
Oct. 2	Shore Co.	Oct. 2	2/10,n/60	√	3,200	3,200		
5	Brown Sup.	Oct. 3	n/10,EOM	√	1,300	1,300		
15	Shore Co.	Oct. 15	2/10,n/60	√	3,990	3,990		
15	Sunshine Co	Oct. 15	2/10,n/60	√	2,650	2,650		

				Cash Receipts Journal					Page 3
Date	Account Credited	PR	Explanation	Cash Dr.	Sales Disc. Dr.	Accts. Rec. Cr.	Sales Cr.	Other Accts. Cr.	COGS Dr. Merch. Inv. Cr.
2014									
Oct. 2	B. Grigsby	√	Inv. 09/23	4,116	84	4,200			
15	Sales		Cash sales	38,830			38,830		21,400
15	M. Craig	√	Inv. 10/6	2,401	49	2,450			

				Cash Disbursements Journal				Page 4
Date	Ch. No.	Payee	Account Debited	PR	Cash Cr.	Merch. Inventory Cr.	Other Accounts Dr.	Accounts Payable Dr.
2014								
Oct. 2	619	Omni Realty	Rent Exp.	640	2,250		2,250	
6	620	Fireside Co.	Fireside Co.	√	3,724	76		3,800
12	621	Shore Co.	Shore Co.	√	3,136	64		3,200
15	622	Jamie Green	Sales Sal. Exp.	621	2,020		2,020	

GENERAL JOURNAL

Page 2

Date		Account Titles and Explanation	PR	Debit	Credit
2014					
Oct.	4	Accounts Payable—Fireside Company	201/√	460	
		Merchandise Inventory	119		460
		Received a credit memo for returns.			
	9	Sales Returns and Allowances	414	850	
		Accounts Receivable—Marge Craig	106/√		850
		Issued a credit memorandum.			
	9	Merchandise Inventory	119	430	
		Cost of Goods Sold	502		430
		Merchandise returned to inventory.			

ACCOUNTS RECEIVABLE SUBLEDGER

Marge Craig

DATE		EXPLANATION	PR	DEBIT	CREDIT	BALANCE
2014						
Oct.	6		S3	3,300		3,300
	9		G2		8,50	2,450
	15		CR3		2,450	-0-

Vickie Foresman

DATE		EXPLANATION	PR	DEBIT	CREDIT	BALANCE
2014						
Oct.	12		S3	3,650		3,650

Parts 2 and 3

Bill Grigsby

DATE	EXPLANATION	PR	DEBIT	CREDIT	BALANCE
2014					
Sept. 23		S2	4,200		4,200
Oct. 2		CR3		4,200	-0-

Amy Ihrig

DATE	EXPLANATION	PR	DEBIT	CREDIT	BALANCE
2014					
Oct. 15		S3	3,100		3,100

ACCOUNTS PAYABLE SUBLEDGER

Fireside Company

DATE	EXPLANATION	PR	DEBIT	CREDIT	BALANCE
2014					
Sept. 28		P1		4,260	4,260
Oct. 4		G2	460		3,800
6		CD4	3,800		-0-

Brown Supply Company

DATE	EXPLANATION	PR	DEBIT	CREDIT	BALANCE
2014					
Oct. 5		P2		1,300	1,300

Sunshine Company

DATE	EXPLANATION	PR	DEBIT	CREDIT	BALANCE
2014					
Oct. 15		P2		2,650	2,650

Parts 2 and 3   (Cont'd.)

Shore Company

DATE	EXPLANATION	PR	DEBIT	CREDIT	BALANCE
2014					
Oct. 2		P2		3,200	3,200
12		CD4	3,200		-0-
15		P2		3,990	3,990

Parts 2 and 3   GENERAL LEDGER

Cash   ACCOUNT NO. 101

DATE	EXPLANATION	PR	DEBIT	CREDIT	BALANCE
2014					
Sept. 30	Balance				5,361

Accounts Receivable   ACCOUNT NO. 106

DATE	EXPLANATION	PR	DEBIT	CREDIT	BALANCE
2014					
Sept. 30	Balance				4,200
Oct. 9		G2		850	3,350

Merchandise Inventory   ACCOUNT NO. 119

DATE	EXPLANATION	PR	DEBIT	CREDIT	BALANCE
2014					
Sept. 30	Balance				66,970
Oct. 4		G2		460	66,510
9		G2	430		66,940

Office Supplies
ACCOUNT NO. 124

DATE	EXPLANATION	PR	DEBIT	CREDIT	BALANCE
2014					
Sept. 30	Balance				607

Store Supplies
ACCOUNT NO. 125

DATE	EXPLANATION	PR	DEBIT	CREDIT	BALANCE
2014					
Sept. 30	Balance				346

Store Equipment
ACCOUNT NO. 165

DATE	EXPLANATION	PR	DEBIT	CREDIT	BALANCE
2014					
Sept. 30	Balance				42,129

Accumulated Depreciation, Store Equipment
ACCOUNT NO. 166

DATE	EXPLANATION	PR	DEBIT	CREDIT	BALANCE
2014					
Sept. 30	Balance				9,153

Accounts Payable
ACCOUNT NO. 201

DATE	EXPLANATION	PR	DEBIT	CREDIT	BALANCE
2014					
Sept. 30	Balance				4,260
Oct. 4		G2	460		3,800

Ken Shaw, Capital
ACCOUNT NO. 301

DATE	EXPLANATION	PR	DEBIT	CREDIT	BALANCE
2014					
Sept. 30	Balance				106,200

Ken Shaw, Withdrawals   ACCOUNT NO. 302

DATE	EXPLANATION	PR	DEBIT	CREDIT	BALANCE
2014					

Sales   ACCOUNT NO. 413

DATE	EXPLANATION	PR	DEBIT	CREDIT	BALANCE
2014					

Sales Returns and Allowances   ACCOUNT NO. 414

DATE	EXPLANATION	PR	DEBIT	CREDIT	BALANCE
2014					
Oct. 9		G2	850		850

Sales Discounts   ACCOUNT NO. 415

DATE	EXPLANATION	PR	DEBIT	CREDIT	BALANCE
2014					

Cost of Goods Sold   ACCOUNT NO. 502

DATE	EXPLANATION	PR	DEBIT	CREDIT	BALANCE
2014					
Oct. 9		G2		430	(430)

Sales Salaries Expense   ACCOUNT NO. 621

DATE	EXPLANATION	PR	DEBIT	CREDIT	BALANCE
2014					
Oct. 15		CD4	2,020		2,020

Rent Expense   ACCOUNT NO. 640

DATE	EXPLANATION	PR	DEBIT	CREDIT	BALANCE
2014					
Oct. 2		CD4	2,250		2,250

Utilities Expense   ACCOUNT NO. 690

DATE	EXPLANATION	PR	DEBIT	CREDIT	BALANCE
2014					

Part 4

SASKAN ENTERPRISES
Trial Balance
October 31, 2014

Part 4

SASKAN ENTERPRISES
Schedule of Accounts Receivable
October 31, 2014

SASKAN ENTERPRISES
Schedule of Accounts Payable
October 31, 2014

Problem 7-6A

Sales Journal							Page
Date	Account Debited	Invoice Number	PR	Accounts Receivable Dr. Sales Cr.	PR	Cost of Goods Sold Dr. Merch. Inventory Cr.	

Purchases Journal									Page
Date	Account Credited	Date of Invoice	Terms	PR	Accts. Payable Cr.	PR	Merch. Inventory Dr.	Office Supplies Dr.	Other Accounts Dr.

NOTE: An additional PR column has been added to both journals to facilitate the referencing of inventory entries into the inventory subsidiary ledger.

Inventory Subledger Record – FIFO Perpetual

Date	PR	Purchases	Sales (at cost)	Inventory Balance

Note: An additional PR column has been added to the Inventory Subledger Record to facilitate referencing of inventory entries.

*Problem 7-7A

Part 1   ACCOUNTS RECEIVABLE SUBLEDGER

Paul Abrams   ACCOUNT NO. 106-1

DATE	EXPLANATION	PR	DEBIT	CREDIT	BALANCE

Linda Hobart   ACCOUNT NO. 106-2

DATE	EXPLANATION	PR	DEBIT	CREDIT	BALANCE

Kelly Schaefer   ACCOUNT NO. 106-3

DATE	EXPLANATION	PR	DEBIT	CREDIT	BALANCE

Part 2   **ACCOUNTS PAYABLE SUBLEDGER**

Frank's Supply   ACCOUNT NO. 201-1

DATE	EXPLANATION	PR	DEBIT	CREDIT	BALANCE

Baskin Company   ACCOUNT NO. 201-2

DATE	EXPLANATION	PR	DEBIT	CREDIT	BALANCE

Sprocket Company   ACCOUNT NO. 201-3

DATE	EXPLANATION	PR	DEBIT	CREDIT	BALANCE

	Eau Claire Inc.				ACCOUNT NO. 201-4	
DATE	EXPLANATION	PR	DEBIT	CREDIT	BALANCE	

Part 3

		Sales Journal				Page
Date	Account Debited		Invoice No.	PR	Accounts Receivable Dr. Sales Cr.	

			Cash Receipts Journal					Page
Date	Account Credited	PR	Explanation	Cash Dr.	Sales Disc. Dr.	Accts. Rec. Cr.	Sales Cr.	Other Accts. Cr.

Purchases Journal   Page

Date	Account Credited	Date of Invoice	Terms	PR	Accts. Payable Cr.	Purchases Dr.	Office Supplies Dr.	Other Accts. Dr.

Cash Disbursements Journal   Page

Date	Ch. No.	Payee	Account Debited	PR	Cash Cr.	Purch. Disc. Cr.	Other Accounts Dr.	Accts. Payable Dr.

GENERAL JOURNAL   Page____

Date	Account Titles and Explanation	PR	Debit	Credit

Cash   ACCOUNT NO. 101

DATE	EXPLANATION	PR	DEBIT	CREDIT	BALANCE
2014					
Mar. 31					167,000

Accounts Receivable   ACCOUNT NO. 106

DATE	EXPLANATION	PR	DEBIT	CREDIT	BALANCE

Merchandise Inventory   ACCOUNT NO. 119

DATE	EXPLANATION	PR	DEBIT	CREDIT	BALANCE
2014					
Mar. 31					105,000

Office Supplies   ACCOUNT NO. 124

DATE	EXPLANATION	PR	DEBIT	CREDIT	BALANCE

Store Supplies   ACCOUNT NO. 125

DATE	EXPLANATION	PR	DEBIT	CREDIT	BALANCE

Store Equipment   ACCOUNT NO. 165

DATE	EXPLANATION	PR	DEBIT	CREDIT	BALANCE

Accounts Payable   ACCOUNT NO. 201

DATE	EXPLANATION	PR	DEBIT	CREDIT	BALANCE

Long-Term Notes Payable   ACCOUNT NO. 251

DATE	EXPLANATION	PR	DEBIT	CREDIT	BALANCE
2014					
Mar. 31					167,000

Jeff Newton, Capital   ACCOUNT NO. 301

DATE	EXPLANATION	PR	DEBIT	CREDIT	BALANCE
2014					
Mar. 31					105,000

Sales   ACCOUNT NO. 413

DATE	EXPLANATION	PR	DEBIT	CREDIT	BALANCE

Sales Discounts   ACCOUNT NO. 415

DATE	EXPLANATION	PR	DEBIT	CREDIT	BALANCE

Purchases   ACCOUNT NO. 505

DATE	EXPLANATION	PR	DEBIT	CREDIT	BALANCE

Purchases Discounts   ACCOUNT NO. 506

DATE	EXPLANATION	PR	DEBIT	CREDIT	BALANCE

Purchases Returns and Allowances   ACCOUNT NO. 507

DATE	EXPLANATION	PR	DEBIT	CREDIT	BALANCE

Sales Salaries Expense ACCOUNT NO. 621

DATE	EXPLANATION	PR	DEBIT	CREDIT	BALANCE

Advertising Expense ACCOUNT NO. 655

DATE	EXPLANATION	PR	DEBIT	CREDIT	BALANCE

*NOTE: For Parts 2 and 3, journalizing and posting, continue journalizing the transactions in the journals provided in *Problem 7-7A.*

Part 5

Trial Balance

	Debit	Credit

Schedule of Accounts Receivable

Schedule of Accounts Payable

Special Journal		Subledger	
Sales	S	Accounts Receivable	AR
Purchases....................	P	Accounts Payable	AP
Cash Receipts	CR	Merchandise Inventory .	MI
Cash Disbursements ..	CD	No Effect........................	NE
General Journal...........	G		

Date	Transaction	Special Journal	Subledger
May 1	The owner invested an automobile into the business.		
2	Sold merchandise and received cash.		
3	Purchased merchandise inventory on credit; terms 1/5, n30.		
4	Sold merchandise on credit.		
5	The customer of May 4 returned defective merchandise; the merchandise was scrapped.		
6	Regarding the May 3 purchase, received a credit memorandum from the supplier granting an allowance.		
15	Paid mid-month salaries.		
17	Purchased office supplies on credit; terms n/30.		
19	Paid for the balance owing on the May 3 purchase.		
22	Received payment on the May 4 sale.		
25	Borrowed money from bank.		
29	Purchased merchandise inventory; paid cash.		
30	Accrued interest revenue.		
30	Closed all revenue accounts to the Income Summary account.		

Sales Journal — Page S1

Date	Account Debited	Invoice Number	PR	Accounts Receivable Dr. Sales Cr.	Cost of Goods Sold Dr. Merchandise Inventory Cr.

Cash Receipts Journal — Page CR1

Date	Accounts Credited	PR	Explanation	Cash Dr.	Sales Disc. Dr.	Accts. Rec. Cr.	Sales Cr.	Other Accts. Cr.	COGS Dr. Merch. Inv. Cr.

Purchases Journal — Page P1

Date	Account Credited	Date of Invoice	Terms	PR	Accounts Payable Cr.	Merch. Inventory Dr.	Office Supplies Dr.	Other Accounts Dr.

Cash Disbursements Journal — Page CD1

Date	Ch. No.	Payee	Account Debited	PR	Cash Cr.	Merch. Inventory Cr.	Other Accounts Dr.	Accounts Payable Dr.

GENERAL JOURNAL   Page____

Date	Account Titles and Explanation	PR	Debit	Credit

Problem 7-3B   Parts 2, 3, 5

Part 1   ACCOUNTS RECEIVABLE SUBLEDGER

Kelly Grody   ACCOUNT NO. 106-1

DATE	EXPLANATION	PR	DEBIT	CREDIT	BALANCE

Karen Harden   ACCOUNT NO. 106-2

DATE	EXPLANATION	PR	DEBIT	CREDIT	BALANCE

Paul Kane   ACCOUNT NO. 106-3

DATE	EXPLANATION	PR	DEBIT	CREDIT	BALANCE

Part 2   ACCOUNTS PAYABLE SUBLEDGER

Beech Company   ACCOUNT NO. 201-1

DATE	EXPLANATION	PR	DEBIT	CREDIT	BALANCE

Blackwater Inc.   ACCOUNT NO. 201-2

DATE	EXPLANATION	PR	DEBIT	CREDIT	BALANCE

Poppe's Supply   ACCOUNT NO. 201-3

DATE	EXPLANATION	PR	DEBIT	CREDIT	BALANCE

Sprague Company   ACCOUNT NO. 201-4

DATE	EXPLANATION	PR	DEBIT	CREDIT	BALANCE

Part 3

				Sales Journal	Page 3
Date	Account Debited	Invoice Number	PR	Accounts Receivable Dr. Sales Cr.	Cost of Goods Sold Dr. Merchandise Inventory Cr.

Cash Receipts Journal									Page 3
Date	Account Credited	PR	Explanation	Cash Dr.	Sales Disc. Dr.	Accts. Rec. Cr.	Sales Cr.	Other Accts. Cr.	COGS Dr. Merch. Inv. Cr.

Purchases Journal								Page 3
Date	Account Credited	Date of Invoice	Terms	PR	Accounts Payable Cr.	Merch. Inventory Dr.	Office Supplies Dr.	Other Accounts Dr.

Cash Disbursements Journal								Page 3
Date	Ch. No.	Payee	Account Debited	PR	Cash Cr.	Merch. Inventory Cr.	Other Accounts Dr.	Accounts Payable Dr.

GENERAL JOURNAL   Page____

Date	Account Titles and Explanation	PR	Debit	Credit

Problem 7-4B

Part 1, 4   GENERAL LEDGER

Cash   ACCOUNT NO. 101

DATE	EXPLANATION	PR	DEBIT	CREDIT	BALANCE
2014					
Jun. 30	Balance brought forward				190,000

Accounts Receivable   ACCOUNT NO. 106

DATE	EXPLANATION	PR	DEBIT	CREDIT	BALANCE

Merchandise Inventory   ACCOUNT NO. 119

DATE	EXPLANATION	PR	DEBIT	CREDIT	BALANCE
2014					
Jun. 30	Balance brought forward				334,000

Office Supplies   ACCOUNT NO. 124

DATE	EXPLANATION	PR	DEBIT	CREDIT	BALANCE

Store Supplies   ACCOUNT NO. 125

DATE	EXPLANATION	PR	DEBIT	CREDIT	BALANCE

Store Equipment   ACCOUNT NO. 165

DATE	EXPLANATION	PR	DEBIT	CREDIT	BALANCE

Accounts Payable   ACCOUNT NO. 201

DATE	EXPLANATION	PR	DEBIT	CREDIT	BALANCE

Long-Term Notes Payable   ACCOUNT NO. 251

DATE	EXPLANATION	PR	DEBIT	CREDIT	BALANCE
2014					
Jun. 30	Balance brought forward				334,000

Gene Duncan, Capital   ACCOUNT NO. 301

DATE	EXPLANATION	PR	DEBIT	CREDIT	BALANCE
2014					
Jun. 30	Balance brought forward				190,000

Sales   ACCOUNT NO. 413

DATE	EXPLANATION	PR	DEBIT	CREDIT	BALANCE

Sales Discounts   ACCOUNT NO. 415

DATE	EXPLANATION	PR	DEBIT	CREDIT	BALANCE

Cost of Goods Sold   ACCOUNT NO. 502

DATE	EXPLANATION	PR	DEBIT	CREDIT	BALANCE

Sales Salaries Expense   ACCOUNT NO. 621

DATE	EXPLANATION	PR	DEBIT	CREDIT	BALANCE

Advertising Expense   ACCOUNT NO. 655

DATE	EXPLANATION	PR	DEBIT	CREDIT	BALANCE

NOTE: For Parts 2, 3, and 4, journalizing and posting, continue journalizing the transactions in the accounts provided in Problem 7-3A.

Part 5

DUNCAN INDUSTRIES
Trial Balance
July 31, 2014

	Debit	Credit

DUNCAN INDUSTRIES
Schedule of Accounts Receivable
July 31, 2014

DUNCAN INDUSTRIES
Schedule of Accounts Payable
July 31, 2014

Analysis component:

_____
_____
_____
_____
_____
_____
_____
_____

Problem 7-5B

Part 1

Sales Journal					Page 3
Date	Account Debited	Invoice Number	PR	Accounts Receivable Dr. Sales Cr.	Cost of Goods Sold Dr. Merchandise Inventory Cr.
2014					
Oct. 6	M. Craig	913	√	6,600	3,600
12	H. Flatt	914	√	7,300	4,000
15	A. Izon	915	√	6,200	3,400

Cash Receipts Journal									Page 3
Date	Account Credited	PR	Explanation	Cash Dr.	Sales Disc. Dr.	Accts. Rec. Cr.	Sales Cr.	Other Accts. Cr.	COGS Dr. Merch. Inv. Cr.
2014									
Oct. 2	J. Wildman	√	Inv. 09/23	8,232	168	8,400			
15	Sales		Cash sales	77,660			77,660		42,800
15	M. Craig	√	Inv. 10/6	4,802	98	4,900			

Purchases Journal

Date	Account Credited	Date of Invoice	Terms	PR	Accounts Payable Cr.	Merch. Inventory Dr.	Office Supplies Dr.	Other Accounts Dr.
2014								
Oct. 2	Walters Co.	10/2	2/10,n/60	√	6,400	6,400		
5	Green Supply	10/3	n/10,EOM	√	2,600	2,600		
15	Walters Co.	10/15	2/10,n/60	√	7,980	7,980		
15	Sunshine Co.	10/15	2/10,n/60	√	5,300	5,300		

Page 2 (Purchases Journal)

Cash Disbursements Journal

Date	Ch. No.	Payee	Account Debited	PR	Cash Cr.	Merch. Inventory Cr.	Other Accounts Dr.	Accounts Payable Dr.
2014								
Oct. 2	619	Omni Realty	Rent Exp.	640	4,500		4,500	
6	620	Fireside Co.	Fireside Co.	√	7,448	152		7,600
12	621	Walters Co.	Walters Co.	√	6,272	128		6,400
15	622	Jamie Ford	Sales Sal. Exp.	621	5,240		5,240	

Page 4 (Cash Disbursements Journal)

GENERAL JOURNAL

Date		Account Titles and Explanation	PR	Debit	Credit
2014					
Oct.	4	Accounts Payable—Fireside Company	201/√	920	
		Merchandise Inventory	119		920
		Received a credit memo for returns.			
	9	Sales Returns and Allowances	414	1,700	
		Accounts Receivable—Marge Craig	106/√		1,700
		Issued a credit memorandum.			

ACCOUNTS RECEIVABLE SUBLEDGER

Marge Craig

DATE		EXPLANATION	PR	DEBIT	CREDIT	BALANCE
2014						
Oct.	6		S3	6,600		6,600
	9		G2		1,700	4,900
	15		CR3		4,900	-0-

Heather Flatt

DATE		EXPLANATION	PR	DEBIT	CREDIT	BALANCE
2014						
Oct.	12		S3	7,300		7,300

Amy Izon

DATE	EXPLANATION	PR	DEBIT	CREDIT	BALANCE
2014					
Oct. 15		S3	6,200		6,200

Jan Wildman

DATE	EXPLANATION	PR	DEBIT	CREDIT	BALANCE
2014					
Sept. 23		S2	8,400		8,400
Oct. 2		CR3		8,400	-0-

ACCOUNTS PAYABLE SUBLEDGER

Fireside Company

DATE	EXPLANATION	PR	DEBIT	CREDIT	BALANCE
2014					
Sept. 28		P1		8,520	8,520
Oct. 4		G2	920		7,600
6		CD4	7,600		-0-

Green Supply Company

DATE	EXPLANATION	PR	DEBIT	CREDIT	BALANCE
2014					
Oct. 5		P2		2,600	2,600

Sunshine Company

DATE	EXPLANATION	PR	DEBIT	CREDIT	BALANCE
2014					
Oct. 15		P2		5,300	5,300

Walters Company

DATE	EXPLANATION	PR	DEBIT	CREDIT	BALANCE
2014					
Oct. 2		P2		6,400	6,400
12		CD4	6,400		-0-
15		P2		7,980	7,980

Parts 2 and 3   **GENERAL LEDGER**

Cash   ACCOUNT NO. 101

DATE	EXPLANATION	PR	DEBIT	CREDIT	BALANCE
2014					
Sept. 30	Balance				10,722

Accounts Receivable   ACCOUNT NO. 106

DATE	EXPLANATION	PR	DEBIT	CREDIT	BALANCE
2014					
Sept. 30	Balance				8,400
Oct. 9		G2		1,700	6,700

Merchandise Inventory   ACCOUNT NO. 119

DATE	EXPLANATION	PR	DEBIT	CREDIT	BALANCE
2014					
Sept. 30	Balance				133,940
Oct. 4		G2		920	133,020

Office Supplies   ACCOUNT NO. 124

DATE	EXPLANATION	PR	DEBIT	CREDIT	BALANCE
2014					
Sept. 30	Balance				1,214

Store Supplies   ACCOUNT NO. 125

DATE	EXPLANATION	PR	DEBIT	CREDIT	BALANCE
2014					
Sept. 30	Balance				692

Store Equipment   ACCOUNT NO. 165

DATE	EXPLANATION	PR	DEBIT	CREDIT	BALANCE
2014					
Sept. 30	Balance				84,258

Accumulated Depreciation, Store Equipment   ACCOUNT NO. 166

DATE	EXPLANATION	PR	DEBIT	CREDIT	BALANCE
2014					
Sept. 30	Balance				18,306

Accounts Payable   ACCOUNT NO. 201

DATE	EXPLANATION	PR	DEBIT	CREDIT	BALANCE
2014					
Sept. 30	Balance				8,520
Oct. 4		G2	920		7,600

Marlee Levin, Capital   ACCOUNT NO. 301

DATE	EXPLANATION	PR	DEBIT	CREDIT	BALANCE
2014					
Sept. 30	Balance				212,400

Marlee Levin, Withdrawals   ACCOUNT NO. 302

DATE	EXPLANATION	PR	DEBIT	CREDIT	BALANCE
2014					

Sales   ACCOUNT NO. 413

DATE	EXPLANATION	PR	DEBIT	CREDIT	BALANCE
2014					

Sales Returns and Allowances   ACCOUNT NO. 414

DATE	EXPLANATION	PR	DEBIT	CREDIT	BALANCE
2014					
Oct. 9		G2	1,700		1,700

Sales Discounts   ACCOUNT NO. 415

DATE	EXPLANATION	PR	DEBIT	CREDIT	BALANCE
2014					

Cost of Goods Sold   ACCOUNT NO. 502

DATE	EXPLANATION	PR	DEBIT	CREDIT	BALANCE
2014					

Sales Salaries Expense   ACCOUNT NO. 621

DATE	EXPLANATION	PR	DEBIT	CREDIT	BALANCE
2014					
Oct. 15		CD4	5,240		5,240

Chapter 7   Problem 7-5B (cont'd.)   *Name* _____

Rent Expense   ACCOUNT NO. 640

DATE	EXPLANATION	PR	DEBIT	CREDIT	BALANCE
2014					
Oct. 2		CD4	4,500		4,500

Utilities Expense   ACCOUNT NO. 690

DATE	EXPLANATION	PR	DEBIT	CREDIT	BALANCE
2014					

Part 4

CHINA MOON PRODUCTS
Trial Balance
October 31, 2014

	Debit	Credit

CHINA MOON PRODUCTS
Schedule of Accounts Receivable
October 31, 2014

CHINA MOON PRODUCTS
Schedule of Accounts Payable
October 31, 2014

Problem 7-6B

				Sales Journal		Page 1
Date	Account Debited	Invoice Number	PR	Accounts Receivable Dr. Sales Cr.	PR	Cost of Goods Sold Dr. Merch. Inventory Cr.

					Purchases Journal				Page 1
Date	Account Credited	Date of Invoice	Terms	PR	Accts. Payable Cr.	PR	Merch. Inventory Dr.	Office Supplies Dr.	Other Accounts Dr.

NOTE: An additional PR column has been added to both journals to facilitate the referencing of inventory entries into the inventory subledger.

Inventory Subledger Record – Weighted Average Perpetual

Date	PR	Purchases	Sales (at cost)	Inventory Balance

Note: An additional PR column has been added to the Inventory Subledger Record to facilitate referencing of inventory entries.

*Problem 7-7B

Part 1   ACCOUNTS RECEIVABLE SUBLEDGER

Kelly Grody   ACCOUNT NO. 106-1

DATE	EXPLANATION	PR	DEBIT	CREDIT	BALANCE

Karen Harden   ACCOUNT NO. 106-2

DATE	EXPLANATION	PR	DEBIT	CREDIT	BALANCE

Paul Kane   ACCOUNT NO. 106-3

DATE	EXPLANATION	PR	DEBIT	CREDIT	BALANCE

Part 2   **ACCOUNTS PAYABLE SUBLEDGER**

Beech Company   ACCOUNT NO. 201-1

DATE	EXPLANATION	PR	DEBIT	CREDIT	BALANCE

Blackwater Inc.   ACCOUNT NO. 201-2

DATE	EXPLANATION	PR	DEBIT	CREDIT	BALANCE

Poppe's Supply   ACCOUNT NO. 201-3

DATE	EXPLANATION	PR	DEBIT	CREDIT	BALANCE

Sprague Company   ACCOUNT NO. 201-4

DATE	EXPLANATION	PR	DEBIT	CREDIT	BALANCE

Part 3

Sales Journal				Page 3
Date	Account Debited	Invoice No.	PR	Accounts Receivable Dr. Sales Cr.

Cash Receipts Journal								Page 3
Date	Account Credited	PR	Explanation	Cash Dr.	Sales Disc. Dr.	Accts. Rec. Cr.	Sales Cr.	Other Accts. Cr.

Purchases Journal								Page 3
Date	Account Credited	Date of Invoice	Terms	PR	Accts. Payable Cr.	Purchases Dr.	Office Supplies Dr.	Other Accts. Dr.

Cash Disbursements Journal								Page 3
Date	Ch. No.	Payee	Account Debited	PR	Cash Cr.	Purch. Disc. Cr.	Other Accounts Dr.	Accts. Payable Dr.

GENERAL JOURNAL   Page____

Date	Account Titles and Explanation	PR	Debit	Credit

*Problem 7-8B

Part 1   GENERAL LEDGER

Cash   ACCOUNT NO. 101

DATE	EXPLANATION	PR	DEBIT	CREDIT	BALANCE
2014					
Jun. 30	Balance brought forward				190,000

Accounts Receivable   ACCOUNT NO. 106

DATE	EXPLANATION	PR	DEBIT	CREDIT	BALANCE

Merchandise Inventory   ACCOUNT NO. 119

DATE	EXPLANATION	PR	DEBIT	CREDIT	BALANCE
2014					
Jun. 30	Balance brought forward				334,000

Office Supplies   ACCOUNT NO. 124

DATE	EXPLANATION	PR	DEBIT	CREDIT	BALANCE

Store Supplies   ACCOUNT NO. 125

DATE	EXPLANATION	PR	DEBIT	CREDIT	BALANCE

Store Equipment   ACCOUNT NO. 165

DATE	EXPLANATION	PR	DEBIT	CREDIT	BALANCE

Accounts Payable   ACCOUNT NO. 201

DATE	EXPLANATION	PR	DEBIT	CREDIT	BALANCE

Long-Term Notes Payable   ACCOUNT NO. 251

DATE	EXPLANATION	PR	DEBIT	CREDIT	BALANCE
2014					
Jun. 30	Balance brought forward				334,000

Gene Duncan, Capital   ACCOUNT NO. 301

DATE	EXPLANATION	PR	DEBIT	CREDIT	BALANCE
2014					
Jun. 30	Balance brought forward				190,000

Sales   ACCOUNT NO. 413

DATE	EXPLANATION	PR	DEBIT	CREDIT	BALANCE

Sales Discounts   ACCOUNT NO. 415

DATE	EXPLANATION	PR	DEBIT	CREDIT	BALANCE

Purchases   ACCOUNT NO. 505

DATE	EXPLANATION	PR	DEBIT	CREDIT	BALANCE

Purchase Discounts   ACCOUNT NO. 506

DATE	EXPLANATION	PR	DEBIT	CREDIT	BALANCE

Purchase Returns and Allowances   ACCOUNT NO. 507

DATE	EXPLANATION	PR	DEBIT	CREDIT	BALANCE

Sales Salaries Expense   ACCOUNT NO. 621

DATE	EXPLANATION	PR	DEBIT	CREDIT	BALANCE

Advertising Expense   ACCOUNT NO. 655

DATE	EXPLANATION	PR	DEBIT	CREDIT	BALANCE

NOTE: For Parts 2 and 3, journalizing and posting, continue journalizing the transactions in the accounts provided in *Problem 7-7B.

Part 5

DUNCAN INDUSTRIES
Trial Balance
July 31, 2014

	Debit	Credit

DUNCAN INDUSTRIES
Schedule of Accounts Receivable
July 31, 2014

DUNCAN INDUSTRIES
Schedule of Accounts Payable
July 31, 2014

Alpine Company - Perpetual

Sales Journal					Page 2
Date	Account Debited	Invoice Number	PR	Accounts Receivable Dr. Sales Cr.	Cost of Goods Sold Dr. Merchandise Inventory Cr.

Purchases Journal								Page 2
Date	Account Credited	Date of Invoice	Terms	PR	Accounts Payable Cr.	Merch. Inventory Dr.	Office Supplies Dr.	Other Accounts Dr.

Cash Receipts Journal									Page 2
Date	Account Credited	PR	Explanation	Cash Dr.	Sales Disc. Dr.	Accts. Rec. Cr.	Sales Cr.	Other Accts. Cr.	COGS Dr. Merch. Inv. Cr.

Alpine Company - Perpetual (Continued)

						Cash Disbursements Journal			Page 2
Date	Ch. No.	Payee	Account Debited	PR	Cash Cr.	Merch. Inventory Cr.	Other Accounts Dr.	Accounts Payable Dr.	

GENERAL JOURNAL   Page 3

Date	Account Titles and Explanation	PR	Debit	Credit

GENERAL JOURNAL   Page 3

Date	Account Titles and Explanation	PR	Debit	Credit

Alpine Company - Perpetual (Continued)

Date	Account Titles and Explanation	PR	Debit	Credit

Cash   ACCOUNT NO. 101

DATE	EXPLANATION	PR	DEBIT	CREDIT	BALANCE
2014					
Apr. 30	Balance				50,247

Accounts Receivable   ACCOUNT NO. 106

DATE	EXPLANATION	PR	DEBIT	CREDIT	BALANCE
2014					
Apr. 30	Balance				4,730

Merchandise Inventory   ACCOUNT NO. 119

DATE	EXPLANATION	PR	DEBIT	CREDIT	BALANCE
2014					
Apr. 30	Balance				220,080

Office Supplies   ACCOUNT NO. 124

DATE	EXPLANATION	PR	DEBIT	CREDIT	BALANCE
2014					
Apr. 30	Balance				430

Store Supplies   ACCOUNT NO. 125

DATE	EXPLANATION	PR	DEBIT	CREDIT	BALANCE
2014					
Apr. 30	Balance				2,447

Alpine Company - Perpetual (Continued)

Prepaid Insurance   ACCOUNT NO. 128

DATE	EXPLANATION	PR	DEBIT	CREDIT	BALANCE
2014					
Apr. 30	Balance				3,318

Office Equipment   ACCOUNT NO. 163

DATE	EXPLANATION	PR	DEBIT	CREDIT	BALANCE
2014					
Apr. 30	Balance				22,470

Accumulated Depreciation, Office Equipment   ACCOUNT NO. 164

DATE	EXPLANATION	PR	DEBIT	CREDIT	BALANCE
2014					
Apr. 30	Balance				9,898

Store Equipment   ACCOUNT NO. 165

DATE	EXPLANATION	PR	DEBIT	CREDIT	BALANCE
2014					
Apr. 30	Balance				38,920

Accumulated Depreciation, Store Equipment   ACCOUNT NO. 166

DATE	EXPLANATION	PR	DEBIT	CREDIT	BALANCE
2014					
Apr. 30	Balance				17,556

Alpine Company - Perpetual (Continued)

Accounts Payable   ACCOUNT NO. 201

DATE	EXPLANATION	PR	DEBIT	CREDIT	BALANCE
2014					
Apr. 30	Balance				7,100

Clint Barry, Capital   ACCOUNT NO. 301

DATE	EXPLANATION	PR	DEBIT	CREDIT	BALANCE
2014					
Apr. 30	Balance				308,088

Clint Barry, Withdrawals   ACCOUNT NO. 302

DATE	EXPLANATION	PR	DEBIT	CREDIT	BALANCE
2014					

Sales   ACCOUNT NO. 413

DATE	EXPLANATION	PR	DEBIT	CREDIT	BALANCE

Sales Discounts   ACCOUNT NO. 414

DATE	EXPLANATION	PR	DEBIT	CREDIT	BALANCE

Alpine Company - Perpetual (Continued)

Sales Returns and Allowances   ACCOUNT NO. 415

DATE	EXPLANATION	PR	DEBIT	CREDIT	BALANCE

Cost of Goods Sold   ACCOUNT NO. 502

DATE	EXPLANATION	PR	DEBIT	CREDIT	BALANCE

Depreciation Expense, Office Equipment   ACCOUNT NO. 612

DATE	EXPLANATION	PR	DEBIT	CREDIT	BALANCE

Depreciation Expense, Store Equipment   ACCOUNT NO. 613

DATE	EXPLANATION	PR	DEBIT	CREDIT	BALANCE

Office Salaries Expense   ACCOUNT NO. 620

DATE	EXPLANATION	PR	DEBIT	CREDIT	BALANCE

Alpine Company - Perpetual (Continued)

Sales Salaries Expense

ACCOUNT NO. 621

DATE	EXPLANATION	PR	DEBIT	CREDIT	BALANCE

Insurance Expense

ACCOUNT NO. 637

DATE	EXPLANATION	PR	DEBIT	CREDIT	BALANCE

Rent Expense, Office Space

ACCOUNT NO. 641

DATE	EXPLANATION	PR	DEBIT	CREDIT	BALANCE

Rent Expense, Selling Space

ACCOUNT NO. 642

DATE	EXPLANATION	PR	DEBIT	CREDIT	BALANCE

Office Supplies Expense

ACCOUNT NO. 650

DATE	EXPLANATION	PR	DEBIT	CREDIT	BALANCE

Alpine Company - Perpetual (Continued)

Store Supplies Expense
ACCOUNT NO. 651

DATE	EXPLANATION	PR	DEBIT	CREDIT	BALANCE
2014					

Utilities Expense
ACCOUNT NO. 690

DATE	EXPLANATION	PR	DEBIT	CREDIT	BALANCE
2014					

Income Summary
ACCOUNT NO. 901

DATE	EXPLANATION	PR	DEBIT	CREDIT	BALANCE

ACCOUNTS RECEIVABLE LEDGER

NAME   Deaver Corp.

DATE	EXPLANATION	PR	DEBIT	CREDIT	BALANCE

NAME   Essex Company

DATE	EXPLANATION	PR	DEBIT	CREDIT	BALANCE

NAME   Nabors, Inc.

DATE	EXPLANATION	PR	DEBIT	CREDIT	BALANCE
2014					
Apr. 28		S2	4,730		4,730

Alpine Company - Perpetual (Continued)

NAME   Oscar Services.

DATE	EXPLANATION	PR	DEBIT	CREDIT	BALANCE
2014					

ACCOUNTS PAYABLE LEDGER

NAME   Chandler Corp.

DATE	EXPLANATION	PR	DEBIT	CREDIT	BALANCE
2014					

NAME   Gale, Inc.

DATE	EXPLANATION	PR	DEBIT	CREDIT	BALANCE
2014					

NAME   Parkay Products

DATE	EXPLANATION	PR	DEBIT	CREDIT	BALANCE
2014					
Apr. 29		P2		7,100	7,100

NAME   Thompson Supply Co.

DATE	EXPLANATION	PR	DEBIT	CREDIT	BALANCE

Alpine Company - Perpetual (Continued)

Alpine Company
Work Sheet
For Month Ended May 31, 2014

Account Titles	Trial Balance		Adjustments		Income Statement		Balance Sheet and Statement of Changes in Equity	
	Debit	Credit	Debit	Credit	Debit	Credit	Debit	Credit

Alpine Company - Perpetual (Continued)

Alpine Company			
Income Statement			
For Month Ended May 31, 2014			

Alpine Company - Perpetual (Continued)

Alpine Company
Statement of Changes in Equity
For Month Ended May 31, 2014

Alpine Company
Balance Sheet
May 31, 2014

Alpine Company - Perpetual (Concluded)

Alpine Company
Post-Closing Trial Balance
May 31, 2014

	Debit	Credit

Alpine Company
Schedule of Accounts Receivable
May 31, 2014

Alpine Company
Schedule of Accounts Payable
May 31, 2014

Alpine Company - Periodic

Sales Journal				Page 2
Date	Account Debited	Invoice Number	PR	Accts. Receivable Dr. Sales Cr.

Purchases Journal								Page 2
Date	Account Credited	Date of Inv.	Terms	PR	Accts. Pay. Cr.	Purchases Dr.	Office Supplies Dr.	Other Accts. Dr.

Cash Receipts Journal							Page 2
Date	Accounts Credited	Explanation	PR	Cash Dr.	Sales Disc. Dr.	Accts. Rec. Cr.	Sales Cr.	Other Accts. Cr.

Alpine Company - Periodic (Continued)

Cash Disbursements Journal								**Page 2**
Date	Ch. No.	Payee	Account Debited	PR	Cash Cr.	Purch. Disc. Cr.	Other Accts. Dr.	Accts. Payable Dr.

GENERAL JOURNAL   Page 3

Date	Account Titles and Explanation	PR	Debit	Credit

Alpine Company - Periodic (Continued)

	GENERAL JOURNAL			Page 3
Date	Account Titles and Explanation	PR	Debit	Credit

Alpine Company - Periodic (Continued)

GENERAL LEDGER

Cash — ACCOUNT NO. 101

DATE	EXPLANATION	PR	DEBIT	CREDIT	BALANCE
2014					
Apr. 30	Balance				50,247

Accounts Receivable — ACCOUNT NO. 106

DATE	EXPLANATION	PR	DEBIT	CREDIT	BALANCE
2014					
Apr. 30	Balance				4,730

Merchandise Inventory — ACCOUNT NO. 119

DATE	EXPLANATION	PR	DEBIT	CREDIT	BALANCE
2014					
Apr. 30	Balance				220,080

Office Supplies — ACCOUNT NO. 124

DATE	EXPLANATION	PR	DEBIT	CREDIT	BALANCE
2014					
Apr. 30	Balance				430

Store Supplies — ACCOUNT NO. 125

DATE	EXPLANATION	PR	DEBIT	CREDIT	BALANCE
2014					
Apr. 30	Balance				2,447

Chapter 7 Comprehensive Problem   *Name* _____

Alpine Company - Periodic (Continued)

Prepaid Insurance ACCOUNT NO. 128

DATE	EXPLANATION	PR	DEBIT	CREDIT	BALANCE
2014					
Apr. 30	Balance				3,318

Office Equipment ACCOUNT NO. 163

DATE	EXPLANATION	PR	DEBIT	CREDIT	BALANCE
2014					
Apr. 30	Balance				22,470

Accumulated Depreciation, Office Equipment ACCOUNT NO. 164

DATE	EXPLANATION	PR	DEBIT	CREDIT	BALANCE
2014					
Apr. 30	Balance				9,898

Store Equipment ACCOUNT NO. 165

DATE	EXPLANATION	PR	DEBIT	CREDIT	BALANCE
2014					
Apr. 30	Balance				38,920

Accumulated Depreciation, Store Equipment ACCOUNT NO. 166

DATE	EXPLANATION	PR	DEBIT	CREDIT	BALANCE
2014					
Apr. 30	Balance				17,556

Alpine Company - Periodic (Continued)

Accounts Payable   **ACCOUNT NO. 201**

DATE	EXPLANATION	PR	DEBIT	CREDIT	BALANCE
20141					
Apr. 30	Balance				7,100

Clint Barry, Capital   **ACCOUNT NO. 301**

DATE	EXPLANATION	PR	DEBIT	CREDIT	BALANCE
2014					
Apr. 30	Balance				308,088

Clint Barry, Withdrawals   **ACCOUNT NO. 302**

DATE	EXPLANATION	PR	DEBIT	CREDIT	BALANCE
2014					

Sales   **ACCOUNT NO. 413**

DATE	EXPLANATION	PR	DEBIT	CREDIT	BALANCE

Sales Discounts   **ACCOUNT NO. 414**

DATE	EXPLANATION	PR	DEBIT	CREDIT	BALANCE

Sales Returns and Allowances   **ACCOUNT NO. 415**

DATE	EXPLANATION	PR	DEBIT	CREDIT	BALANCE

Alpine Company - Periodic (Continued)

Purchases   ACCOUNT NO. 505

DATE	EXPLANATION	PR	DEBIT	CREDIT	BALANCE

Purchases Discounts   ACCOUNT NO. 506

DATE	EXPLANATION	PR	DEBIT	CREDIT	BALANCE

Purchases Returns and Allowances   ACCOUNT NO. 507

DATE	EXPLANATION	PR	DEBIT	CREDIT	BALANCE

Depreciation Expense, Office Equipment   ACCOUNT NO. 612

DATE	EXPLANATION	PR	DEBIT	CREDIT	BALANCE

Depreciation Expense, Store Equipment   ACCOUNT NO. 613

DATE	EXPLANATION	PR	DEBIT	CREDIT	BALANCE

Office Salaries Expense   ACCOUNT NO. 620

DATE	EXPLANATION	PR	DEBIT	CREDIT	BALANCE

Alpine Company - Periodic (Continued)

Sales Salaries Expense — ACCOUNT NO. 621

DATE	EXPLANATION	PR	DEBIT	CREDIT	BALANCE

Insurance Expense — ACCOUNT NO. 637

DATE	EXPLANATION	PR	DEBIT	CREDIT	BALANCE

Rent Expense, Office Space — ACCOUNT NO. 641

DATE	EXPLANATION	PR	DEBIT	CREDIT	BALANCE

Rent Expense, Selling Space — ACCOUNT NO. 642

DATE	EXPLANATION	PR	DEBIT	CREDIT	BALANCE

Office Supplies Expense — ACCOUNT NO. 650

DATE	EXPLANATION	PR	DEBIT	CREDIT	BALANCE

Alpine Company - Periodic (Continued)

Store Supplies Expense   ACCOUNT NO. 651

DATE	EXPLANATION	PR	DEBIT	CREDIT	BALANCE
2014					

Utilities Expense   ACCOUNT NO. 690

DATE	EXPLANATION	PR	DEBIT	CREDIT	BALANCE
2014					

Income Summary   ACCOUNT NO. 901

DATE	EXPLANATION	PR	DEBIT	CREDIT	BALANCE

ACCOUNTS RECEIVABLE LEDGER

NAME   Deaver Corp.

DATE	EXPLANATION	PR	DEBIT	CREDIT	BALANCE

NAME   Essex Company

DATE	EXPLANATION	PR	DEBIT	CREDIT	BALANCE

NAME   Nabors, Inc.

DATE	EXPLANATION	PR	DEBIT	CREDIT	BALANCE
2014					
Apr. 28		S2	4,730		4,730

Alpine Company - Periodic (Continued)

NAME   Oscar Services.

DATE	EXPLANATION	PR	DEBIT	CREDIT	BALANCE
2014					

ACCOUNTS PAYABLE LEDGER

NAME   Chandler Corp.

DATE	EXPLANATION	PR	DEBIT	CREDIT	BALANCE
2014					

NAME   Gale, Inc.

DATE	EXPLANATION	PR	DEBIT	CREDIT	BALANCE
2014					

NAME   Parkay Products

DATE	EXPLANATION	PR	DEBIT	CREDIT	BALANCE
2014					
Apr. 29		P2		7,100	7,100

NAME   Thompson Supply Co.

DATE	EXPLANATION	PR	DEBIT	CREDIT	BALANCE

Alpine Company - Periodic (Continued)

Alpine Company
Work Sheet
For Month Ended May 31, 2014

Account Titles	Trial Balance		Adjustments		Income Statement		Balance Sheet and Statement of Changes in Equity	
	Debit	Credit	Debit	Credit	Debit	Credit	Debit	Credit

Alpine Company - Periodic (Continued)

Alpine Company
Income Statement
For Month Ended May 31, 2014

Alpine Company - Periodic (Continued)

Alpine Company
Statement of Changes in Equity
For Month Ended May 31, 2014

Alpine Company
Balance Sheet
May 31, 2014

Alpine Company - Periodic (Concluded)

Alpine Company
Post-Closing Trial Balance
May 31, 2014

	Debit	Credit

Alpine Company
Schedule of Accounts Receivable
May 31, 2014

Alpine Company
Schedule of Accounts Payable
May 31, 2014

(a) _____

_____

_____

_____

_____

_____

(b) _____

_____

_____

_____

_____

_____

(c) _____

_____

_____

_____

Quick Study 8-2

_____

_____

_____

_____

_____

_____

_____

_____

Quick Study 8-3

a. _____

_____

_____

_____

b. _____

_____

_____

_____

(1) Establishment of the fund:

GENERAL JOURNAL   Page____

Date	Account Titles and Explanation	PR	Debit	Credit

(2) Summary of petty cash receipts and entry to reimburse the fund at month-end:

Wee Ones Agency
Petty Cash Payments Report
May 1 – 31, 2014

Receipts: _____

_____

_____

_____

_____

Fund total

Less: Cash remaining

Equals: Cash required to replenish petty cash

Cash over/(short)

GENERAL JOURNAL   Page____

Date	Account Titles and Explanation	PR	Debit	Credit

(3) _____

_____

_____

_____

GENERAL JOURNAL   Page____

Date	Account Titles and Explanation	PR	Debit	Credit

Quick Study 8-6

GENERAL JOURNAL   Page____

Date	Account Titles and Explanation	PR	Debit	Credit

GENERAL JOURNAL   Page____

Date	Account Titles and Explanation	PR	Debit	Credit

GENERAL JOURNAL   Page____

Date	Account Titles and Explanation	PR	Debit	Credit

Quick Study 8-9   Parts 1 and 2:

	Bank or Book Effect	**Add or Subtract**	**Journal Entry Required or Not**
(a)			
(b)			
(c)			
(d)			
(e)			
(f)			
(g)			

Bank Reconciliation

GENERAL JOURNAL   Page____

Date	Account Titles and Explanation	PR	Debit	Credit

Quick Study 8-11

_____
_____
_____
_____
_____
_____
_____
_____
_____
_____

Exercise 8-2

_____
_____
_____
_____
_____
_____
_____
_____
_____
_____
_____

Exercise 8-3

 (a) _____
_____
_____
_____
_____

(b) _____
_____
_____
_____
_____
_____

Internal Control Problem: _____
_____
_____
_____
_____
_____
_____
_____

Internal Control Recommendation: _____
_____
_____
_____
_____
_____

Exercise 8-5

(a) Establish the Fund

GENERAL JOURNAL   Page____

Date	Account Titles and Explanation	PR	Debit	Credit

(b) Prepare a summary of petty cash receipts

Cameron Co.
Petty Cash Payments Report
January 1 – 8, 2014

Receipts: _____
_____
_____
_____
_____
_____

Fund total _____
Less: Cash remaining _____
Equals: Cash required to replenish petty cash _____
Cash over/(short) _____

Record the reimbursement:

GENERAL JOURNAL   Page____

Date	Account Titles and Explanation	PR	Debit	Credit

Analysis component: _____

_____

_____

_____

_____

Exercise 8-6

(a) Establish the Fund

GENERAL JOURNAL   Page____

Date	Account Titles and Explanation	PR	Debit	Credit

(b) Prepare a summary of petty cash receipts

Willard Company
Petty Cash Payments Report
September 9 – 30, 2014

Receipts: _____

_____
_____
_____
_____
_____

Fund total
Less: Cash remaining
Equals: Cash required to replenish petty cash
Cash over/(short)

Reimburse and reduce the fund

GENERAL JOURNAL   Page_____

Date	Account Titles and Explanation	PR	Debit	Credit

Analysis component:

_____
_____
_____
_____
_____
_____
_____
_____

GENERAL JOURNAL   Page____

Date	Account Titles and Explanation	PR	Debit	Credit
a.				
b.				
c.				

Exercise 8-8

GENERAL JOURNAL   Page____

Date	Account Titles and Explanation	PR	Debit	Credit

GENERAL JOURNAL   Page____

Date	Account Titles and Explanation	PR	Debit	Credit

Exercise 8-9

GENERAL JOURNAL   Page____

Date	Account Titles and Explanation	PR	Debit	Credit

GENERAL JOURNAL   Page____

Date	Account Titles and Explanation	PR	Debit	Credit

Analysis component:

_____
_____
_____
_____
_____
_____
_____
_____
_____

Chapter 8 **Exercise 8-10** *Name* _____

Part 1

Part 2

GENERAL JOURNAL Page____

Date	Account Titles and Explanation	PR	Debit	Credit

Analysis component: _____

Exercise 8-11

a. _____

b.   **GENERAL JOURNAL**   Page____

Date	Account Titles and Explanation	PR	Debit	Credit

Analysis component:

_____

_____

_____

_____

_____

_____

	Bank Balance		Book Balance			Not Shown on the Reconciliation
	Add	Deduct	Add	Deduct	Adjust	
1. Interest earned on the account.						
2. Deposit made on September 30 after the bank was closed.						
3. Cheques outstanding on August 31 that cleared the bank in September.						
4. NSF cheque from customer returned on September 15 but not recorded by the company.						
5. Cheques written and mailed to payees on September 30.						
6. Deposit made on September 5 that was processed on September 8.						
7. Bank service charge.						
8. Cheques written and mailed to payees on October 5.						
9. Cheque written by another depositor but charged against the company's account.						
10. Principal and interest collected by the bank but not recorded by the company.						
11. Special charge for collection of note in No. 10 on company's behalf.						
12. Cheque written against the account and cleared by the bank; not recorded by the bookkeeper.						

	Case X	Case Y	Case Z

(lines for answers)

Problem 8-1A

(1) Principle Violated:
Recommendation:

(2) Principle Violated:
Recommendation:

(3) Principle Violated:
Recommendation:

(4) Principle Violated:
Recommendation:

(5) Principle Violated:
Recommendation:

Part 1   GENERAL JOURNAL   Page____

Date	Account Titles and Explanation	PR	Debit	Credit

Part 2

Milton Consulting
Petty Cash Payments Report
February 2 – 28, 2014

Receipts:

Fund total
Less: Cash remaining
Equals: Cash required to replenish petty cash
Cash over/(short)

Part 3   GENERAL JOURNAL   Page____

Date	Account Titles and Explanation	PR	Debit	Credit

Analysis component: _____

_____
_____
_____
_____
_____
_____
_____

Problem 8-3A

GENERAL JOURNAL   Page____

Date	Account Titles and Explanation	PR	Debit	Credit

Analysis component: _____

_____
_____
_____
_____
_____
_____

a. _____

b.   **GENERAL JOURNAL**   Page____

Date	Account Titles and Explanation	PR	Debit	Credit

Analysis component: _____

_____
_____
_____
_____
_____

Name _____

a.

_____
_____
_____

b.

GENERAL JOURNAL

Page_____

Date	Account Titles and Explanation	PR	Debit	Credit

GENERAL JOURNAL   Page____

Date	Account Titles and Explanation	PR	Debit	Credit

Problem 8-6A

Part 1

Part 2

GENERAL JOURNAL

Page____

Date		Account Titles and Explanation	PR	Debit	Credit

Analysis component: _____

_____

_____

_____

_____

_____

_____

_____

_____

_____

_____

Part 1

Part 2

GENERAL JOURNAL   Page____

Date	Account Titles and Explanation	PR	Debit	Credit

Analysis component: _____

_____
_____
_____
_____
_____
_____
_____
_____
_____
_____

Problem 8-8A

a. _____

_____

b.   **GENERAL JOURNAL**   Page____

Date	Account Titles and Explanation	PR	Debit	Credit

Problem 8-9A

a. _____

b.   **GENERAL JOURNAL**   Page____

Date	Account Titles and Explanation	PR	Debit	Credit

Problem 8-10A

Part 1

Part 2

GENERAL JOURNAL   Page____

Date	Account Titles and Explanation	PR	Debit	Credit

Analysis component:

_____

_____

_____

_____

_____

_____

(1) Principle Violated:

     Recommendation:

(2) Principle Violated:

     Recommendation:

(3) Principle Violated:

     Recommendation:

(4) Principle Violated:

     Recommendation:

(5) Principle Violated:

     Recommendation:

Part 1   GENERAL JOURNAL   Page____

Date	Account Titles and Explanation	PR	Debit	Credit

Part 2

Stihl Repairs
Petty Cash Payments Report
July 5 – 31, 2014

Receipts:

Fund total
Less: Cash remaining
Equals: Cash required to replenish petty cash
Cash over/(short)

Part 3   GENERAL JOURNAL   Page____

Date	Account Titles and Explanation	PR	Debit	Credit

Analysis component: _____
_____
_____
_____
_____
_____
_____
_____

Problem 8-3B

GENERAL JOURNAL

Page____

Date	Account Titles and Explanation	PR	Debit	Credit

Analysis component: _____
_____
_____
_____
_____
_____

a.

_____

b.   **GENERAL JOURNAL**   Page____

Date	Account Titles and Explanation	PR	Debit	Credit

Analysis component: _____

_____
_____
_____
_____
_____
_____
_____

a.

_____

_____

b. _____   **GENERAL JOURNAL**   Page____

Date	Account Titles and Explanation	PR	Debit	Credit

Part 1

_____

_____

Part 2

GENERAL JOURNAL   Page_____

Date	Account Titles and Explanation	PR	Debit	Credit

Analysis component: _____

_____
_____
_____
_____
_____
_____
_____
_____
_____

Problem 8-7B   Part 1

_____
_____

Part 2   **GENERAL JOURNAL**   Page____

Date	Account Titles and Explanation	PR	Debit	Credit

GENERAL JOURNAL   Page____

Date	Account Titles and Explanation	PR	Debit	Credit

Analysis component:

_____
_____
_____
_____
_____
_____
_____
_____
_____
_____

Problem 8-8B   Part 1

_____
_____

Part 2   **GENERAL JOURNAL**   Page____

Date	Account Titles and Explanation	PR	Debit	Credit

Problem 8-9B   Part 1

Part 2   GENERAL JOURNAL   Page____

Date	Account Titles and Explanation	PR	Debit	Credit

Problem 8-10B   Part 1

_____

_____

Part 2

GENERAL JOURNAL   Page____

Date	Account Titles and Explanation	PR	Debit	Credit

Analysis component: _____

_____

_____

_____

_____

_____

GENERAL JOURNAL

Date	Account Titles and Explanation	PR	Debit	Credit

Quick Study 9-2

GENERAL JOURNAL

Date	Account Titles and Explanation	PR	Debit	Credit

GENERAL JOURNAL

Date	Account Titles and Explanation	PR	Debit	Credit

Quick Study 9-3

Biatech
Partial Balance Sheet
December 31, 2014

GENERAL JOURNAL

Date	Account Titles and Explanation	PR	Debit	Credit

Quick Study 9-5

Allowance for Doubtful Accounts

GENERAL JOURNAL   Page____

Date	Account Titles and Explanation	PR	Debit	Credit

Quick Study 9-6

a.   ## GENERAL JOURNAL   Page____

Date	Account Titles and Explanation	PR	Debit	Credit

b. _____

c. _____

GENERAL JOURNAL   Page____

Date	Account Titles and Explanation	PR	Debit	Credit

Allowance for Doubtful Accounts

Quick Study 9-8

GENERAL JOURNAL   Page____

Date	Account Titles and Explanation	PR	Debit	Credit

Quick Study 9-9

GENERAL JOURNAL   Page____

Date	Account Titles and Explanation	PR	Debit	Credit

GENERAL JOURNAL

Date	Account Titles and Explanation	PR	Debit	Credit

Quick Study 9-11

GENERAL JOURNAL

Date	Account Titles and Explanation	PR	Debit	Credit

*Quick Study 9-12

GENERAL JOURNAL

Date	Account Titles and Explanation	PR	Debit	Credit

GENERAL JOURNAL

Date		Account Titles and Explanation	PR	Debit	Credit

Calculations:

_____
_____
_____
_____
_____
_____

*Quick Study 9-14

a. _____
b. _____
c. _____

Part 1

GENERAL LEDGER

Accounts Receivable	Sales	Sales Returns and Allowances

ACCOUNTS RECEIVABLE SUBLEDGER

ABC Shop	Colt Enterprises	Red McKenzie

Part 2

<u>Comparison:</u>

GENERAL JOURNAL

Date	Account Titles and Explanation	PR	Debit	Credit

Exercise 9-3

GENERAL JOURNAL

Date	Account Titles and Explanation	PR	Debit	Credit

a.

Accounts Receivable	Allowance for Doubtful Accounts

GENERAL JOURNAL

Date	Account Titles and Explanation	PR	Debit	Credit

b.

Accounts Receivable	Allowance for Doubtful Accounts

GENERAL JOURNAL

Date	Account Titles and Explanation	PR	Debit	Credit

Exercise 9-5

a. _____

b. _____

c. _____

d. _____

e. _____

_____
Partial Balance Sheet
_____

Exercise 9-7

a, b, and c   **GENERAL JOURNAL**   Page____

Date	Account Titles and Explanation	PR	Debit	Credit

a, b, and c (cont'd.)   GENERAL JOURNAL   Page_____

Date	Account Titles and Explanation	PR	Debit	Credit

Calculations:

Accounts Receivable	Allowance for Doubtful Accounts

d.

Partial Balance Sheet		

Analysis component:

_____

_____

_____

_____

_____

_____

a, b, and c.   **GENERAL JOURNAL**   Page____

Date	Account Titles and Explanation	PR	Debit	Credit

Calculations:

Accounts Receivable	**Allowance for Doubtful Accounts**

d.

Partial Balance Sheet

Analysis component:

_____

_____

_____

_____

_____

Exercise 9-9

a and b.   **GENERAL JOURNAL**   Page____

Date	Account Titles and Explanation	PR	Debit	Credit

Calculations:

Accounts Receivable   **Allowance for Doubtful Accounts**

Chapter 9   Exercise 9-9 (concl'd.)   *Name* _____

c.

_____
                        Partial Balance Sheet
_____

Analysis component:

_____
_____
_____
_____
_____

Exercise 9-10

                        GENERAL JOURNAL   Page____

Date	Account Titles and Explanation	PR	Debit	Credit

Analysis component:

_____
_____
_____
_____
_____
_____
_____

GENERAL JOURNAL

Date	Account Titles and Explanation	PR	Debit	Credit

Exercise 9-12

GENERAL JOURNAL

Date	Account Titles and Explanation	PR	Debit	Credit

GENERAL JOURNAL

Date	Account Titles and Explanation	PR	Debit	Credit

GENERAL JOURNAL

Date	Account Titles and Explanation	PR	Debit	Credit

Financial Statement Note(s):

_____

_____

_____

_____

Name _____

GENERAL JOURNAL

Date	Account Titles and Explanation	PR	Debit	Credit

Calculations:

_____
_____
_____
_____
_____
_____

*Exercise 9-16

Part 1

    Accounts Receivable Turnover   **Days' Sales Uncollected**

_____
_____
_____
_____
_____
_____
_____

Part 2

_____
_____
_____
_____
_____
_____
_____
_____

a. **Expense is 2% of credit sales:**

GENERAL JOURNAL

Date	Account Titles and Explanation	PR	Debit	Credit

b. **Allowance is 5% of accounts receivable:**

GENERAL JOURNAL

Date	Account Titles and Explanation	PR	Debit	Credit

Calculations for Part b:

Allowance for
Doubtful Accounts

Part 2

Part 3

Analysis component:

_____

_____

_____

_____

_____

Chapter 9   Problem 9-2A   Part 1   *Name* _____

Calculation of the required balance of the allowance (using an aging analysis):

_____
_____
_____
_____
_____
_____
_____
_____

Allowance for Doubtful Accounts

Part 2

GENERAL JOURNAL

Date	Account Titles and Explanation	PR	Debit	Credit

Analysis component:

_____
_____
_____
_____
_____
_____

Part 1   GENERAL JOURNAL   Page____

Date	Account Titles and Explanation	PR	Debit	Credit

Part B
Part 2   GENERAL JOURNAL   Page____

Date		Account Titles and Explanation	PR	Debit	Credit

Part 3

		Debit	Credit

Part 4

_____

_____

Part C
Part 5   GENERAL JOURNAL   Page____

Date		Account Titles and Explanation	PR	Debit	Credit

Calculations:

Accounts Receivable	Allowance for Doubtful Accounts

Part 6

	Debit	Credit

Part 7

_____

_____

Name _____

GENERAL JOURNAL

Date	Account Titles and Explanation	PR	Debit	Credit
2014				
a.				
b.				
c.				
d.				

Calculations:

Accounts Receivable   **Allowance for Doubtful Accounts**

GENERAL JOURNAL

Date	Account Titles and Explanation	PR	Debit	Credit
2015				
e.				
f.				
g.				
h.				

Calculations:

Accounts Receivable

Allowance for Doubtful Accounts

Part 1
Part a.

GENERAL JOURNAL

Date	Account Titles and Explanation	PR	Debit	Credit
2014				

Allowance for Doubtful Accounts

Part b.

Part 2
Part c.

GENERAL JOURNAL

Date	Account Titles and Explanation	PR	Debit	Credit
2014				

Calculations:

Allowance for Doubtful Accounts

Part d.

Name _____

Part 1

GENERAL JOURNAL

Date	Account Titles and Explanation	PR	Debit	Credit

Part 2

GENERAL JOURNAL

Date	Account Titles and Explanation	PR	Debit	Credit

Calculations:

Accounts Receivable		Allowance for Doubtful Accounts	

Problem 9-7A

a.

Month

Customer	Not yet due 0.5%	1 to 29 days past due 1%	30 to 59 days past due 4%	60 to 89 days past due 10%	90 to 119 days past due 20%	Over 119 days past due 50%
B. Axley						
T. Holton						
W. Nix						
C. Percy						
K. Willis						

b.   **GENERAL JOURNAL**   Page____

Date	Account Titles and Explanation	PR	Debit	Credit

Calculations:

Accounts Receivable	Allowance for Doubtful Accounts

Problem 9-8A

a.   **GENERAL JOURNAL**   Page____

Date	Account Titles and Explanation	PR	Debit	Credit
2014				
2015				
2016				

Calculations:

Accounts Receivable		Allowance for Doubtful Accounts	

Analysis component:

_____
_____
_____
_____
_____

Problem 9-9A

Parts a, b, and c.

Date of Note	Principal	Interest Rate	Term	Maturity Date	Days of Accrued Interest at Dec. 31, 2014	Accrued Interest at Dec. 31, 2014
Nov. 1/13	$240,000	4%	180 days			
Jan. 5/14	$100,000	5%	90 days			
Nov. 20/14	$90,000	4.5%	45 days			
Dec. 10/14	$120,000	5.5%	30 days			

Calculations:

_____
_____
_____
_____
_____
_____
_____
_____
_____
_____
_____
_____
_____
_____

d. <div align="center">GENERAL JOURNAL</div>   Page____

Date	Account Titles and Explanation	PR	Debit	Credit

e. <div align="center">GENERAL JOURNAL</div>   Page____

Date	Account Titles and Explanation	PR	Debit	Credit

Problem 9-10A

a. <div align="center">GENERAL JOURNAL</div>   Page____

Date	Account Titles and Explanation	PR	Debit	Credit

GENERAL JOURNAL   Page____

Date	Account Titles and Explanation	PR	Debit	Credit

b. Determine the maturity date of the note dated March 2:

_____
_____
_____
_____
_____
_____

Prepare the entry on the maturity date:

GENERAL JOURNAL   Page____

Date	Account Titles and Explanation	PR	Debit	Credit

Parts (a) to (f)

GENERAL JOURNAL   Page____

Date	Account Titles and Explanation	PR	Debit	Credit

Analysis component:

_____

_____

_____

_____

_____

_____

GENERAL JOURNAL   Page____

Date	Account Titles and Explanation	PR	Debit	Credit

Analysis component: _____

_____

_____

_____

_____

GENERAL JOURNAL   Page____

Date	Account Titles and Explanation	PR	Debit	Credit

GENERAL JOURNAL   Page____

Date	Account Titles and Explanation	PR	Debit	Credit

a. Expense is 3% of credit sales:

GENERAL JOURNAL

Date	Account Titles and Explanation	PR	Debit	Credit

b. Allowance is 6% of accounts receivable:

GENERAL JOURNAL

Date	Account Titles and Explanation	PR	Debit	Credit

Calculations for Part b:

Allowance for Doubtful Accounts

Part 2

Part 3

Analysis component:

Calculation of the required balance of the allowance (using an aging analysis):

_____
_____
_____
_____
_____
_____
_____

Allowance for Doubtful Accounts

Part 2

GENERAL JOURNAL

Date	Account Titles and Explanation	PR	Debit	Credit

Analysis component:

_____
_____
_____
_____
_____
_____

Part 1   **GENERAL JOURNAL**   Page____

Date	Account Titles and Explanation	PR	Debit	Credit

Part B
Part 2   GENERAL JOURNAL   Page_____

Date	Account Titles and Explanation	PR	Debit	Credit

Part 3

			Debit	Credit

Part 4

_____

Part C
Part 5   GENERAL JOURNAL   Page_____

Date	Account Titles and Explanation	PR	Debit	Credit

Calculations:

Accounts Receivable	Allowance for Doubtful Accounts

Part 6

		Debit	Credit

Part 7

_____

GENERAL JOURNAL

Date	Account Titles and Explanation	PR	Debit	Credit
2014				
a.				
b.				
c.				
d.				

Calculations:

Accounts Receivable	Allowance for Doubtful Accounts

GENERAL JOURNAL

Date	Account Titles and Explanation	PR	Debit	Credit
2015				
e.				
f.				
g.				
h.				

Calculations:

Accounts Receivable   Allowance for Doubtful Accounts

Name _____

Part a

GENERAL JOURNAL

Date	Account Titles and Explanation	PR	Debit	Credit
2014				

Allowance for Doubtful Accounts

Part b

Part c

GENERAL JOURNAL

Date	Account Titles and Explanation	PR	Debit	Credit
2014				

Calculations:

Allowance for Doubtful Accounts

Part d

Part 1

GENERAL JOURNAL

Date		Account Titles and Explanation	PR	Debit	Credit

Part 2

GENERAL JOURNAL

Date		Account Titles and Explanation	PR	Debit	Credit

Calculations:

Accounts Receivable	Allowance for Doubtful Accounts

Problem 9-7B

a.

Month

Customer	Not yet due 1.5%	1 to 29 days past due 2%	30 to 59 days past due 5%	60 to 89 days past due 20%	90 to 119 days past due 35%	Over 119 days past due 50%
A. Leslie						
T. Meston						
P. Obrian						
L. Timms						
W. Victor						

b.   GENERAL JOURNAL   Page____

Date	Account Titles and Explanation	PR	Debit	Credit

Calculations:

Accounts Receivable	Allowance for Doubtful Accounts

Problem 9-8B

a.   GENERAL JOURNAL   Page____

Date	Account Titles and Explanation	PR	Debit	Credit
2014				
2015				
2016				

Calculations:

Accounts Receivable	Allowance for Doubtful Accounts

Analysis component:

_____
_____
_____
_____
_____

Problem 9-9B

Parts a, b, and c.

Date of Note	Principal	Interest Rate	Term	Maturity Date	Days of Accrued Interest at Dec. 31, 2014	Accrued Interest at Dec. 31, 2014
Sept. 20/13	$490,000	3%	120 days			
June 01/14	$240,000	3.5%	45 days			
Nov. 23/14	$164,000	4.5%	90 days			
Dec. 18/14	$120,000	4%	30 days			

Calculations:

_____
_____
_____
_____
_____
_____
_____
_____
_____
_____
_____
_____
_____
_____
_____

d.   **GENERAL JOURNAL**   Page____

Date	Account Titles and Explanation	PR	Debit	Credit

e.   **GENERAL JOURNAL**   Page____

Date	Account Titles and Explanation	PR	Debit	Credit

Problem 9-10B

a.   **GENERAL JOURNAL**   Page____

Date	Account Titles and Explanation	PR	Debit	Credit

GENERAL JOURNAL   Page____

Date	Account Titles and Explanation	PR	Debit	Credit

b. Determine the maturity date of the note dated March 1:

_____

_____

_____

_____

_____

_____

Prepare the entry on the maturity date:

GENERAL JOURNAL   Page____

Date	Account Titles and Explanation	PR	Debit	Credit

Parts (a) to (f)

GENERAL JOURNAL   Page____

Date	Account Titles and Explanation	PR	Debit	Credit

Analysis component: _____
_____
_____
_____
_____
_____

GENERAL JOURNAL   Page____

Date	Account Titles and Explanation	PR	Debit	Credit

Analysis component:

_____
_____
_____
_____
_____

GENERAL JOURNAL

Page____

Date	Account Titles and Explanation	PR	Debit	Credit

GENERAL JOURNAL

Page____

Date	Account Titles and Explanation	PR	Debit	Credit

_____
_____
_____
_____
_____
_____
_____

Quick Study A-2

GENERAL JOURNAL

Date	Account Titles and Explanation	PR	Debit	Credit

Quick Study A-3

GENERAL JOURNAL

Date	Account Titles and Explanation	PR	Debit	Credit

Quick Study A-4

		Deductions				Pay	Distribution	
Employee	Gross Pay	EI Premium	Taxes	CPP	Deductions Total	Net Pay	Office Salaries	Sales Salaries
Johnson, S.	1,200.00	21.96	266.95	56.07				
Waverley, N.	530.00	9.70	63.30	22.90				
Zender, B.	675.00	12.35	98.15	30.08				
Totals	2,405.00	44.01	428.40	109.05				

Name _____

Employee	Gross Pay	Deductions				Pay	Salaries Expense
		EI Premium	Taxes	CPP	Total Deductions	Net Pay	
Bentley, A.	2,010.00						
Craig, T.	2,115.00						
Totals	4,125.00						

Quick Study A-6

Employee	Gross Pay	Deductions				Pay	Distribution	
		EI Premium	Income Taxes	CPP	Total Deductions	Net Pay	Office Salaries	Sales Salaries
Withers, S.	2,500.00						2,500.00	
Volt. C.	1,800.00							1,800.00
Totals	4,300.00							

Calculations:

_____

_____

_____

_____

_____

_____

_____

_____

Quick Study A-7

GENERAL JOURNAL   Page____

Date	Account Titles and Explanation	PR	Debit	Credit

GENERAL JOURNAL

Date	Account Titles and Explanation	PR	Debit	Credit

Quick Study A-9

GENERAL JOURNAL

Date	Account Titles and Explanation	PR	Debit	Credit

Quick Study A-10

GENERAL JOURNAL

Date	Account Titles and Explanation	PR	Debit	Credit

GENERAL JOURNAL

Date		Account Titles and Explanation	PR	Debit	Credit

Exercise A-1

Exercise A-2

Employee	Gross Pay	Deductions					Pay
		EI Premium	Income Taxes	CPP	Health Insurance	Total Deductions	Net Pay
H. Chea	720.00		115.50		24.00		
J. Lim	610.00		88.30		24.00		
D. Patelli	830.00		148.95		36.00		
S. Quinata	1,700.00		460.70		24.00		
Totals	3,860.00		813.45		108.00		

Calculations:

_____
_____
_____
_____
_____
_____
_____

Name _____

GENERAL JOURNAL

Date	Account Titles and Explanation	PR	Debit	Credit

Exercise A-3

Employee	Gross Pay	EI Prem.	Income Taxes	United Way	CPP	Total Deductions	Net Pay	Admin. Salaries	Sales Salaries
Akerley, D.	1,900.00	34.77	381.95	80.00	87.39				
Nesbitt, M.	1,260.00	23.06	187.95	50.00	55.71				
Trent, F.	1,680.00	30.74	304.85	40.00	76.50				
Vacon, M.	3,000.00	54.90	768.50	300.00	141.84				
Totals	7,840.00	143.47	1,643.25	470.00	361.44				

Exercise A-4

Employee	Gross Pay	EI Prem.	Income Taxes	Canada Savings Bonds	CPP	United Way	Total Deductions	Net Pay	Office Salaries	Sales Salaries
Crimson	1,995.00								1,995.00	
Long	2,040.00									2,040.00
Morris	2,000.00									2,000.00
Peterson	2,280.00									2,280.00
Totals	8,315.00									

Appendix I   Exercise A-5   *Name* _____

Employee	Gross Pay	EI Prem.	Income Taxes	Medical Ins.	CPP	United Way	Total Deductions	Net Pay	Office Salaries	Guide Salaries
				Deductions				**Payment**	**Distribution**	
Wynne	1,200.00			65.00		40.00				1,200.00
Short	950.00			65.00		100.00			950.00	
Pearl	1,150.00			65.00		0				1,150.00
Quince	875.00			65.00		50.00				875.00
Totals	4,175.00									

Calculations:

_____
_____
_____
_____
_____
_____
_____
_____

Exercise A-6

_____
_____
_____
_____
_____
_____
_____

GENERAL JOURNAL

Date	Account Titles and Explanation	PR	Debit	Credit

GENERAL JOURNAL

Date	Account Titles and Explanation	PR	Debit	Credit

Exercise A-8

GENERAL JOURNAL

Date	Account Titles and Explanation	PR	Debit	Credit

Exercise A-9

GENERAL JOURNAL

Date	Account Titles and Explanation	PR	Debit	Credit

GENERAL JOURNAL

Date		Account Titles and Explanation	PR	Debit	Credit

Exercise A-11

Employee	CPP Contribution	EI Contribution	Retirement Fund Contributions	Health Insurance

Calculations:

_____
_____
_____
_____
_____
_____
_____
_____
_____
_____
_____

GENERAL JOURNAL

Date	Account Titles and Explanation	PR	Debit	Credit

Exercise A-13

GENERAL JOURNAL

Date	Account Titles and Explanation	PR	Debit	Credit

Appendix I Problem A-1A *Name* _____

Part 1

Employee	M	T	W	T	F	S	S	Total Hrs.	O.T. Hrs.	Reg. Pay Rate	Regular Pay	O.T. Premium Pay	Gross Pay
			Daily Time									Earnings	
Loran	8	8	8	8	8	4	0			40.00			
Sousa	7	8	6	7	8	4	0			36.00			
Smith	8	8	0	8	8	4	4			32.00			
Parton	8	8	8	8	8	0	0			40.00			
Wood	0	6	6	6	6	8	8			36.00			

Employee	EI Prem.	CPP	Income Tax	Hosp. Ins.	Union Dues	Total Deductions	Net Pay	Office Salaries Expense	Service Wages Expense
	Deductions						Payment	Distribution	
Loran				40.00	16.00				
Sousa				40.00	15.00				
Smith				40.00	14.00				
Parton				40.00	16.00				
Wood				40.00	15.00				
Totals				200.00	76.00				

Part 2

GENERAL JOURNAL

Date	Account Titles and Explanation	PR	Debit	Credit

Part 1

GENERAL JOURNAL

Date	Account Titles and Explanation	PR	Debit	Credit

Part 2

GENERAL JOURNAL

Date	Account Titles and Explanation	PR	Debit	Credit

Problem A-3A

Part 1

GENERAL JOURNAL

Date	Account Titles and Explanation	PR	Debit	Credit

Appendix I   Problem A-3A (concl.)   *Name* _____

Part 2

GENERAL JOURNAL

Date	Account Titles and Explanation	PR	Debit	Credit

Part 3

GENERAL JOURNAL

Date	Account Titles and Explanation	PR	Debit	Credit

Problem A-4A

GENERAL JOURNAL

Date	Account Titles and Explanation	PR	Debit	Credit

GENERAL JOURNAL

Date	Account Titles and Explanation	PR	Debit	Credit

Part 1

Employee	Daily Time							Total Hrs.	O.T. Hrs.	Reg. Pay Rate	Earnings		
	M	T	W	T	F	S	S				Regular Pay	O.T. Premium Pay	Gross Pay
Amoko	8	8	8	8	8	0	0			34.00			
Carson	7	8	8	7	8	4	0			36.00			
De	8	8	0	8	8	4	4			36.00			
Deszca	8	8	8	8	8	0	0			30.00			
Tan	0	6	6	6	6	8	8			30.00			

Employee	Deductions						Payment	Distribution	
	EI Prem.	CPP	Income Tax	Hosp. Ins.	Union Dues	Total Deductions	Net Pay	Office Wages Expense	Service Wages Expense
Amoko				30.00	12.00				
Carson				30.00	12.00				
De				30.00	12.00				
Deszca				30.00	12.00				
Tan				30.00	12.00				
Totals				150.00	60.00				

Part 2

GENERAL JOURNAL

Date	Account Titles and Explanation	PR	Debit	Credit

Part 1

GENERAL JOURNAL

Date		Account Titles and Explanation	PR	Debit	Credit

Part 2

GENERAL JOURNAL

Date		Account Titles and Explanation	PR	Debit	Credit

Problem A-3B

Part 1

GENERAL JOURNAL

Date		Account Titles and Explanation	PR	Debit	Credit

Part 2

GENERAL JOURNAL

Date	Account Titles and Explanation	PR	Debit	Credit

Part 3

GENERAL JOURNAL

Date	Account Titles and Explanation	PR	Debit	Credit

Problem A-4B

GENERAL JOURNAL

Date	Account Titles and Explanation	PR	Debit	Credit

GENERAL JOURNAL

Date	Account Titles and Explanation	PR	Debit	Credit